Library Service
to Tweens

Library Service to Tweens

MELANIE A. LYTTLE *and*
SHAWN D. WALSH

McFarland & Company, Inc., Publishers
Jefferson, North Carolina

ISBN (print) 978-1-4766-6319-7
ISBN (ebook) 978-1-4766-2574-4

LIBRARY OF CONGRESS CATALOGUING DATA ARE AVAILABLE

BRITISH LIBRARY CATALOGUING DATA ARE AVAILABLE

Front cover photograph © 2017 kate_sept2004/iStock

Printed in the United States of America

*McFarland & Company, Inc., Publishers
Box 611, Jefferson, North Carolina 28640
www.mcfarlandpub.com*

To the children and tweens of Madison Public Library
for inspiring us to always provide the best library
experience possible.
To our families for all their love and support.

Acknowledgments

We know that people often skip the acknowledgments, but we wanted to include one anyway. There are many people who in one way or another made this book possible, and publicly thanking them is important to us.

We'll start with a huge thank you to the Lawrence, Moran and Wade families. Without their oldest children being loyal library patrons from when they started attending Li-Beary Babes at ten months old, we wouldn't have begun to wonder how to keep them loyal patrons of the library as they were growing older and becoming tweens. Likewise, without these children, we never would have embarked on the journey of tween services, and this book would never have come to be. The parents of these children trusted us to take care of them, and when we asked these parents to allow their children to form the core of our first tween advisory group when they were barely tweens, they said yes. We cannot thank you enough.

An extra thank you to JD because, without you, Miss Melanie would have known nothing about Pokémon. Your confidence that she would be able to get what was needed for the library if she just followed your directions means more to her than you will ever know.

Thanks to the entire staff at Madison Public Library in Madison, Ohio. We experiment all the time with different program ideas and arrangements for the collection. We try different outreach locations and apply for grants to get someone else to pay for our experiments. You have celebrated our successes with us and consoled us during failures. An extra shout-out goes to Dawn Weaver, Deanna Bottar, Jenny Vernyi, and Nick Mayer, who are also part of the current team providing materials and programs for tweens.

Thank you to Nancy Currie, our director, as well as our library board. Your support has been so important to us. We could not do what we do if we did not have your backing.

Thank you to Carrie Svigel, president of the Friends of Madison Public Library, and all those who donate their time and talents to Friends activities. The money you raise ultimately gets returned to the library through monetary donations for special programs like tween lock-ins. We really appreciate your support.

Finally, thank you to Janet Ingraham Dwyer, Amanda L.S. Murphy, and Robyn Vittek for giving us feedback as we worked on the manuscript. You helped us convey our message as clearly and completely as possible.

Table of Contents

Introduction

The Importance of Talking about Tweens in the Library

Currently there is very little information available on tween library services. It is helpful to everyone in the field to share the successes, failures, and learnings that come from providing services to this changeable and often perplexing group of patrons. Through exchanging knowledge, library staff can gain confidence and knowledge to provide exceptional tween library services.

There are plenty of amazing articles and blog postings about tween services, and they give a wealth of good things to think about. There are also libraries that have parts of their websites devoted to "Teen and Tween Services." But where is the "how to" book? Ideally, this book answers that question. Our goal is to help others organize their thoughts about what tween services in their community will look like. This present work is designed to move through a variety of areas to create a smooth, logical progression of developing tween library services.

As authors, we never imagined that we would write about library services for tweens. However, we both believe that we have in our community some of the most amazing, caring, awesome tweens ever, and they deserve the best from their library. Providing those library services is what we do. Through this book, we share our learnings and observations.

Part of the magic of tween library services, and what makes this area unlike any other in the library, is that it frequently does not follow any patterns or preconceived ideas. The needs of tweens vary from community to community. Tweens are always evolving, and everywhere unique. Looking back, developing tween services at our library was a messy and chaotic process. From designing programming to creating a separate tween materials collection to simply trying to figure out who was a tween in the community, nothing has been as straightforward as we hope it will be for readers of this book.

Tweens deserve their own spaces and services, and some of them expect it. If readers are fortunate enough to have children growing up in libraries and believing *their* library should serve them and their needs, then they're off to a great start. However, pioneering tween services as a library can be lonely. This book is intended to show such intrepid pioneers that there are others who have been there and want to offer help and advice.

Our final word before proceeding is that we have made mistakes, and so will you. Learn from our mistakes and learn from your own. Mistakes are not failures, but opportunities to learn and to do better in the future.

SECTION I

Who Is a Tween?

The next four chapters will lay the groundwork for who tweens are. Looking from several different angles, we can develop a clear picture of this ever-changing group of people.

The first chapter is a very broad overview of relevant developmental and educational psychology concepts that relate to the people called "tweens." For some readers, this information will represent only a small percentage of what they already know about this age group, gleaned from previous study and course work. For others, this information will be brand new. In order to create a common starting point for a discussion of library services for tweens, however, it is necessary for everyone to begin in about the same place.

The second chapter looks at available writings on tweens. The one thing that most people can agree on about tweens, in all their diversity, is that, relatively speaking, not much is written about them. The bulk of what is written comes from a marketing perspective, since tweens attract more attention in terms of writing and research as a group of potential consumers. The education and library fields have some information about tweens, but certainly not the volume that comes from marketing.

The third chapter takes the broad descriptions of tweens gleaned from the first two chapters and makes this information a bit more specific by looking at tween archetypes. These are sweeping generalizations, but they do take into account many earlier aspects of what has been learned about tweens. This chapter begins to bring the idea of tweens back from a theoretical level to a more practical level regarding what can be observed in the library.

The final chapter in this section is about examining the community to determine who tweens are in specific locales. Through the first three chapters, it becomes clear that there is no way to accurately describe all tweens all the time. At best, generalizations can be made about what tweens are like. However, librarians in specific communities know their tweens and community members best, and this knowledge is what will make tween services successful at their libraries.

1

Developmental and Educational Psychology

The discussion of tweens begins by looking at who they are from an educational and developmental psychology perspective. However, to begin the immersion into the world of tweens, it makes sense to consider tweens' most common method for searching for information, aside from asking their peers: they "google" it or use whatever web browser is at hand. Their search methods often bring up *Wikipedia* articles and things that many librarians might question as being the most reputable and reliable sources of information. However, growing up in this world of constant connectedness, with everything being on the Internet, significantly influences who tweens are. They are an ever-evolving and difficult-to-describe group of individuals.

Wikipedia will serve as a great resource throughout this stage of research for reasons other than being what tweens use. Once upon a time, the *World Book Encyclopedia*, shelved in the reference section of practically every library, was the first place people went to get a broad understanding of a topic or idea. That encyclopedia seemed to have at least a little bit of information on everything. Now, however, *Wikipedia* has for many people become the "go-to" source for clear, concise explanations of complicated topics. Another advantage to *Wikipedia* is that someone is updating, adding, or clarifying entries all the time. Whether librarians want to admit it or not, *Wikipedia* is also fairly reliable (to a certain point), and often offers easy routes to further exploration of a topic. With these ideas in mind, the topics and ideas that are touched on briefly in the following pages have been described in much detail on *Wikipedia*, but not in a way that is so esoteric as to be impossible to understand.

In their broadest sense, tweens can be described as whatever anyone wants to define them as being; depending on a person's perspective, that can be a broad range of ages between eight and fifteen. However, different communities or groups of people may label tweens as a narrower group. A library's definition of who counts as a tween will come from its community. In this book we will use a broad age range in the hopes that it will provide the most useful information for the most people. Not everyone coming to the library profession will have had the opportunity to learn about developmental psychology, and probably far fewer have read educational psychology. However, having a general idea of some of the major ideas from these areas will help develop a picture of who are tweens in a particular community. Library professionals are encouraged to research and follow their own interests in particular elements of developmental psychology or to look further into particular scientists who are mentioned. However, the idea here is to provide a general overview.

Definitions

To begin the discussion of tweens with some definitions, the first comes courtesy of the *Learner's Dictionary*, which defines a tween as "a boy or girl who is 11 or 12 years old." Using that definition, there is a very limited age range for tweens. Another online dictionary, Dictionary.com, provides a slightly different definition: "[a tween is] a youngster between 10 and 12 years of age, considered too old to be a child and too young to be a teenager." This begins the challenge: Does a person become a tween starting at ten years old or eleven?

Since definitions for the word *tween* are not especially clear-cut, the word *adolescence* may be more enlightening. According to Merriam-Webster.com, "adolescence'" is "the period of life from puberty to maturity terminating legally at the age of majority." Returning to Dictionary.com to look up the same word, the definition is fairly similar. This source defines adolescence as "the transitional period between puberty and adulthood in human development, extending mainly over the teen years and terminating legally when the age of majority is reached." Judging from these two definitions, it appears that adolescence does not have an exact age because it begins at puberty and continues until a person is eighteen—the age of majority.

Since the word *puberty* is used in the previous definition, does it appear that there is an age range for that? Starting with Merriam-Webster.com, puberty is "the period of life when a person's sexual organs mature and he or she becomes able to have children ... the age at which puberty occurs often construed legally as 14 in boys and 12 in girls." Perhaps a medical answer for the definition of puberty is advisable. That may also provide some information to add to the definition of *tween*. This is one from *WebMD*, since that seems to be a place that many people rely on for their medical information: "Puberty usually begins in girls around ages 8 to 13 and in boys between 10 and 15. In girls, normal changes include breast development, body hair growth, and starting your first period. In boys, puberty brings about changes such as genital growth, body hair growth, increase in height, and a deeper voice" ("Puberty Directory," WebMD.com). This medical definition of puberty finally gives a broad age range for a physical change that happens within humans. Comparing the dictionary and medical definitions of puberty, there are definite differences.

Looking at the terms *tween, adolescence,* and *puberty,* a definition of tweens can be created. For the purposes of this book, *tweens* will be defined as children somewhere between 9 and 14 years of age, the time when boys and girls go through puberty (roughly fourth through eighth grade). Another way to describe this would be to say that one is a tween when the physical and hormonal changes occur that result in a transition from childhood to adolescence. A third, more colloquial way of describing tweens would be to call them individuals who cannot decide if they want to be a child or an adult, so they change from moment to moment.

Now, having designated an age range for tweens, it is easier to look at some other aspects of those ages from a developmental psychology perspective.

Developmental Psychology

Looking at what developmental psychology is exactly begins with a definition from *Wikipedia*, which describes it as the "scientific study of how and why human beings change over the course of their life" ("Developmental Psychology," 2015). Having the opportunity look at how different scientists view the change in humans as they mature will provide more information to use in describing the nature of tweens as well as looking at how tweens learn and acquire information.

Jean Piaget

Jean Piaget is most famous for his theory of cognitive development. According to this theory, there are certain stages that humans go through on the way to maturity, even though it is a continuous process of developing, learning, and changing. Piaget identifies four distinct stages of development: sensorimotor, preoperational, concrete operational, and formal operational. Using the general age range of tweens, the concrete and formal operational stages are encompassed for this time period. For the concrete operational stage, the general age range is 7–11 years, and the formal operational stage is from 11 to at least 15 years old, and possibly up to 20 years.

The youngest tweens are in the concrete operational stage. They are beginning to use logical thought. They are really looking at very concrete things, as opposed to theoretical notions, but they can reason through certain ideas and sometimes come to conclusions about things. Even more noteworthy, they are now able to look at perspectives other than their own. There is no arguing that the rise of selfies and social media may be causing people to become more egocentric as they mature instead of less; however, Piaget asserts that children in this stage are becoming less focused on only themselves and beginning to apply logic to solving at least concrete problems (but not abstract ones).

Older tweens are in the formal operational stage of development. This is characterized by the ability to think abstractly. It is also when people develop the ability for metacognition, which not only allows people to evaluate their thoughts but also brings to mind the stubbornly popular meme and phrase "that's so meta." Being logical in solving problems instead of just using a trial-and-error method is key to this stage of development. Overall, the formal operational stage is characterized by logical thought, but there is still egocentric thought and behavior. This social thinking has two types: imaginary audience, which involves a person using attention-getting behavior, and personal fable, in which people develop and act on their own sense of being unique and invincible ("Piaget's Theory of Cognitive Development").

Erik Erikson

Erik Erikson is famous for developing the idea of states of psychosocial development, which go from infancy to adulthood. He studied with Anna Freud, daughter of Sigmund Freud, so his ideas are somewhat influenced by Freudian thinking as well as his own experiences growing up. Erikson describes eight stages of development, with his fourth and fifth stages being applicable to tweens. The fourth state is competence, in which tweens ask the question, "Can I make it in the world of people and things?" and that occurs from 5 to 12 years old; the fifth state is fidelity, which involves asking the question, "Who am I and what can I be?" and that occurs from 13 to 19 years old ("Erikson's Stages of Psychosocial Development."). These two stages cover a lot of developmental growth, so this explains why the tween years can be so turbulent and exciting at the same time.

Erikson's stage of competence, which is also described by the question of industry versus inferiority, covers most of elementary school, and sometimes, instead of an age span, it is labeled as (elementary) school age. However, looking at the 5-to-12-year-old age span, most tweens will be within this range. But Erikson does say that development is very fluid, and tweens may not spend a majority of their time in this phase.

Returning to what the competency stage entails, there are similarities to other developmental theories. Erikson talks about people at this stage seeing themselves as individuals with the ability to solve problems and accomplish tasks independently. The idea of being independent can mean that some exhibited behaviors are rebellious, but people in this stage are developing self-confidence and their image of who they are. This stage is also characterized by people developing their own interests and wanting to follow them, as well as sadness if they are not allowed to develop and explore who they are and what they are good at.

For the oldest tweens, the fidelity stage (also described as identity versus role confusion) encompasses ages 13 to 19. This stage is characterized by a worry of how one appears to others. It is also about questioning where one fits within the world of adults or within society as a whole. There can be a lot of experimenting (as well as arguing and rebelling) in this stage, as people are trying to see what they like and where they fit in. This stage is characterized by great changes, both physical and mental. Deciding where one belongs in the world and how other people relate to him or her sets up the adult developmental stages that come later.

Abraham Maslow

While Abraham Maslow is famous for his hierarchy of needs, generally there are not ages attached to these levels. However, when looking at tweens, it is worthwhile to consider these stages because they are still phases of growth and human development. Tweens will fluctuate across most of the levels as other factors in their life influence how they act and think.

The most basic level in the hierarchy is physiological needs—things necessary for a body to function. These include water, food, clothing, and shelter. Certainly in libraries, staff sees tweens whose basic needs have not been met. Without that foundation, there will not be any progress beyond the first level. The second level is safety needs. This includes personal and physical safety, and it can be especially influential with children. For an adult, this may include other types of safety, but it is noted that for children the safety needs can be particularly important. The third stage is loving and belonging. This is all interpersonal, and sometimes it is even more important to children than safety ("Maslow's Hierarchy of Needs"). This level describes how people create relationships with others. They want to feel accepted by social groups. In addition to love, this level can also deal with peer pressure. The fourth stage is esteem—being respected by others and having self-respect. Sometimes the need for respect from others is followed by the need for self-respect and self-esteem. The final level is self-actualization, which is generally believed to happen in adulthood. This is about determining and realizing one's full potential. More than likely tweens are moving between the lower four levels of the hierarchy.

Lawrence Kohlberg

Lawrence Kohlberg is famous for developing stages of moral development. His work is an outgrowth of Piaget's theory. However, like Maslow's hierarchy, there are not definite ages associated with Kohlberg's stages. There are six stages of moral development, and while tweens are unlikely to go beyond the fourth stage, looking at them all is worthwhile in order to more fully understand tweens.

The first two stages of moral development are called the pre-conventional stages and are most common in children. These stages are based on evaluating the morality of an action solely on its direct consequences. What will happen to the person based on a specific action? Such decision making is egocentric and without regard for the conventions of any greater organizations. Stage 1 is about obedience and punishment. If there will be a punishment, then the action is wrong. The second stage focuses on self-interest. This is when decisions are made and acted upon if it is right for the person involved. These decisions are based on rewards ("Lawrence Kohlberg's Stages of Moral Development").

The third and fourth stages of moral development are called conventional, and they tend to be common in adolescents and adults. This is the time when people believe in and abide by societal norms and rules of behavior, sometimes blindly. The third stage of moral development is characterized by trying to abide by and function within social standards. The person wants to be viewed by others as a good person, and he/she chooses behaviors that will support that view by others. The fourth stage involves looking at the social order and maintaining it. This is about adhering to rules and laws, which is very important individually and for society as a whole.

Educational Psychology

Arguably there are several connections between developmental and educational psychology. Many librarians view themselves as educators regardless of whether they are formally trained. Toward this end, the definition of a tween will include information from educational psychology. To begin, educational psychology is the discipline that examines the behavioral and cognitive influences that affect how people learn, allowing "researchers to understand individual differences in intelligence, cognitive development, affect, motivation, self-regulation, and self-concept, as well as their role in learning" ("Educational Psychology").

Constructivism

Jean Piaget is now mentioned a second time, as he was the founder of constructivism. This philosophy of education emphasizes play and exploration as important to learning. While much can be said about specific elements of this philosophy, the key point is the idea of incorporating new experiences into a person's existing knowledge and framework. Additionally, if the new information or experiences do not fit the existing framework, then a new structure must be created to accommodate the new information. That is one of the reasons why Piaget saw play as the important work of children because this was how they gained new knowledge. This is very much about learning by doing ("Constructivism").

Zone of Proximal Development

Lev Vygotsky used the term *zone of proximal development* (ZPD) to describe how children learn. He took a different approach than the constructivists and other major developmental theorists, for he believed that "through the assistance of a more capable person, a child is able to learn skills or aspects of a skill that go beyond the child's actual developmental or maturational level. Therefore, development always follows the child's potential to learn" ("Lev Vygotsky"). For librarians, this is connected to providing quality materials and programs for tweens to learn from. It is also about having great staff to help tweens mature and progress. The proper term within this idea is *scaffolding*, and while the creation of this term is credited to Jerome Bruner, it is closely associated with Vygotsky and the zone of proximal development. Librarians can take this information and look at it from a more concrete illustration: "Scaffolding is a process through which a teacher or a more competent peer helps the student in his or her ZPD as necessary and tapers off this aid as it becomes unnecessary, much as a scaffold is removed from a building after construction is completed" ("Zone of Proximal Development"). This is collaboration and exploration.

Bloom's Taxonomy

Benjamin Bloom created his taxonomy to improve education. According to this theory, educational tasks can be broken up into smaller tasks that check for knowledge, comprehension, application, analysis, synthesis, and evaluation. The idea was that these evaluation tools were discrete and measurable. Oftentimes *higher-order thinking* is a term used to talk about how some skills, like demonstrating knowledge and comprehension, are less complicated than showing synthesis or evaluation of information. Interestingly enough, Bloom's taxonomy (especially its description of higher-order thinking) can work with the idea of multiple intelligences, outlined below ("Bloom's Taxonomy").

Theory of Multiple Intelligences

Howard Gardner is credited with bringing the theory of multiple intelligences to the forefront in the 1980s. It describes intelligence as being a collection of behavioral criteria. These different intelligences include musical-rhythmic and harmonic, visual-spatial, verbal-linguistic, logical-mathematical, bodily-kinesthetic, interpersonal, intrapersonal, and naturalistic. Some still question whether Gardner's theory creates a better, broader definition of intelligence or whether it merely swaps the words *ability* and *intelligence* ("Theory of Multiple Intelligences"). However, this theory suggests that wide variety within programs and offerings for tweens will be helpful for their development and maturity.

The Takeaway from the Chapter

The research outlined above demonstrates that the tween period of development is filled with many changes, so that one tween will be very different from another. Putting together all this information, a picture of an amazing period of time in the life of a tween emerges. There are so many things to discover and learn. Tweens are on the cusp of deciding who they will be as adults, and that is part of what makes being a librarian for tweens so rewarding.

A tween is:

- a male or female between the ages of 9 and 14;
- about to or currently going through puberty, at which time many physical changes are occurring;
- also going through a tremendous period of intellectual and experiential growth;

- evolving from only using limited logical thought to being fully able to reason through questions and problems;
- egocentric, but more in the sense that people are looking at him or her, and not that he or she is the only person in the world;
- able to see that other people have other ways of seeing the world;
- thinking about how he or she thinks and views the rest of the world;
- focusing on becoming independent and doing things on his or her own;
- investigating what hobbies and interests seem most appealing and enjoyable;
- discovering that he or she has aptitudes for certain activities and areas in school;
- very concerned with how other people perceive him or her;
- sometimes more concerned about being safe within a family group or location than even having food and shelter;
- looking to make sure that he or she is accepted into a social group or family;
- hoping to belong somewhere and to develop a bond with likeminded people;
- easily swayed by peer pressure because being respected by others is important;
- changing his or her behavior from acting solely out of self-interest and avoiding punishment to working within the norms of society;
- trying to abide by the rules of society for the greater good;
- trying to accumulate as many different experiences as possible;
- learning, exploring, and pushing the boundaries of his or her world;
- able to accomplish much more with the help of more knowledgeable adults or peers than can be accomplished alone;
- taking his or her learning from play and formal instruction and displaying that learning in many different ways; and
- able to think and learn in many different ways and has many different abilities that are unique and special.

REFERENCES

"Adolescence." (n.d.). Dictionary.com. Retrieved from http://dictionary.reference.com/browse/adolescence.

"Adolescence." (n.d.). *Merriam-Webster.com.* Retrieved from http://www.merriam-webster.com/dictionary/adolescence.

"Bloom's taxonomy." *Wikipedia.* https://en.wikipedia.org/wiki/Bloom%27s_taxonomy (retrieved December 11, 2015).

"Constructivism (philosophy of education)." *Wikipedia.* https://en.wikipedia.org/wiki/Constructivism_ (philosophy_of_education) (retrieved November 21, 2015).

"Developmental psychology." *Wikipedia.* https://en.wikipedia.org/wiki/Developmental_psychology (retrieved December 11, 2015).

"Educational psychology." *Wikipedia.* https://en.wikipedia.org/wiki/Educational_psychology (retrieved December 8, 2015).

"Erikson's stages of psychosocial development. *Wikipedia.* https://en.wikipedia.org/wiki/Erikson%27s_ stages_of_psychosocial_development (retrieved December 12, 2015).

"Lawrence Kohlberg's stages of moral development." *Wikipedia.* https://en.wikipedia.org/wiki/ Lawrence_Kohlberg%27s_stages_of_moral_development (retrieved December 11, 2015).

"Lev Vygotsky." *Wikipedia.* https://en.wikipedia.org/wiki/Lev_Vygotsky (retrieved November 28, 2015).

1. Development and Education Psychology of Tweens

"Maslow's hierarchy of needs." *Wikipedia.* https://en.wikipedia.org/wiki/Maslow%27s_hierarchy_of_ needs#Research (retrieved September 15, 2015).

"Piaget's theory of cognitive development." *Wikipedia.* https://en.wikipedia.org/wiki/Piaget%27s_ theory_of_cognitive_development (retrieved December 10, 2015).

"Puberty." *Merriam-Webster.com.* Retrieved from http://www.merriam-webster.com/dictionary/ puberty.

"Puberty directory." *WebMD.* Retrieved from http://teens.webmd.com/puberty-directory.

"Theory of multiple intelligences." *Wikipedia.* https://en.wikipedia.org/wiki/Theory_of_multiple_intel- ligences (retrieved December 11, 2015).

"Tween." Dictionary.com. Retrieved from http://dictionary.reference.com/browse/tween?s=t.

"Tween." *Learner's Dictionary.* Retrieved from http://www.learnersdictionary.com/definition/tween.

"Zone of proximal development." *Wikipedia.* https://en.wikipedia.org/wiki/Zone_of_proximal_ development (retrieved December 9, 2015).

2

Current Writings on Tweens

Since there is not a widely accepted age range for tweens, finding research on this group can be difficult. However, defining an age range for tweens does not appear to be the only reason why there is little information available about them. Looking at what is available provides a beginning for the discussion: What are tweens like? Many different researchers and authors examine that question from different angles, creating another dimension of the tween profile.

There are three basic areas that information about tweens seems to center around. First, there is the educational and scientific perspective, generally regarding how tweens learn or behave in school. In addition, there are starting to be more articles in the library world about serving tweens there; these tend to be primarily focused on programming. Finally, there are articles that refer to marketing products to tweens, which can come from the popular media as well as marketing focused publications. Each area brings a little bit more information to bear on the tween profile.

Education and Science

Generally, when the leaders and experts of the education and science realms talk about tweens, they are talking about middle school or junior high school students. They are in between the elementary and high school grades. This narrower definition of tweens still provides information that can be applicable to a slightly broader age range.

In the article "Differentiating for Tweens," Rick Wormeli gives different strategies for teaching middle-school-age tweens. His suggestions can be applied to how tween librarians both create programs and market materials to this age group. He talks about "seven conditions that young adolescents crave: competence and achievement; opportunities for self-definition; creative expression; physical activity; positive social interactions with adults and peers; structure and clear limits; and meaningful participation in family school, and community" (Wormeli, 2006). The idea that tweens want to define who they are, as well as be creative and active, points to the types of activities that can be successful in the library. Wanting structure and limits speaks to the idea of providing discipline and routine within activities. Finally, meaningful participation looks to the types of activities that tweens engage in, as well as giving them the opportunity to make contributions to the library.

2. Current Writings on Tweens

In "Stories from Tween Classrooms," Bruce Morgan and Deb Odom reflect on the writing abilities of fourth- and sixth-grade students. While libraries generally concentrate on reading, how tweens process writing and synthesize what they learn points to types of books that could be good matches for them. Particularly noteworthy is the fact that these seasoned teachers recognize tweens as a mass of contradictions: "Tweens are unpredictable. They go from being young adults to babbling infants in a second. One moment they are introspective and thoughtful; the next, they howl with laughter at an inappropriate remark. They look deeply into the meaning of text, and then grab their Pokémon cards and head to recess" (Morgan and Odom, 2006). This takes into account the widely varying developmental levels of this life stage, as mentioned in the first chapter.

Taking a look at solely the information-seeking behavior of tweens, the article "Cognitive Authority in Everyday Life" directly addresses something that librarians work with extensively: helping tweens find reliable information. Tweens know that adults tend to be reputable sources of information, but they do not always go there for answers. Instead, "information services need to build emotional support for asking questions, not just provide authoritative answers" (Meyers, 2010). This article speaks to the need for tween librarians, and truly all library reference staff, to show empathy and compassion for tweens, or they will not be asked for help in locating information and answers. Making that personal connection is vital to tweens.

Brain and hormonal changes are the focus of the article by Richard M. Marshall and Sharon Neuman titled "Brain Changes from Tween to Teen." In reading about the attention-seeking and risky behaviors described as happening in school, many librarians will recognize variants happening within their buildings. However, "except for the period from birth to age 3 or 4, there is no other time when so many changes occur so rapidly" (Marshall and Neuman, 2012). Children's librarians are used to working with very young children whose development proceeds rapidly, but tween librarians are working with patrons who are changing just as much. Helping tweens make good choices and reinforcing the boundaries and rules of the library will help tweens have more successful experiences there.

Looking at these four articles, as well as other, similar articles, several themes recur. First, the changeable nature of tweens is undeniable. They will be docile and adorable one minute, and then obstinate and annoying in the next second. However, this is their development at work. The need to provide clear boundaries for tweens, as for most children, is also repeated. However, with tweens, these boundaries are both providing for their safety and security and offering them something to depend on as so much of their world is changing. Providing this authority as clearly and calmly as possible will make library experiences successful and ensure that the tweens will come back and ask for more help because the authority is sensitive but firm. There is no condescension or value judgment involved. A person who shows respect to and interest in tweens is someone whom they will trust with their information needs, which is, of course, what librarians want. These articles mention (in different ways) that it takes a special kind of person to be a teacher of tweens, and the same can be said about being a tween librarian.

The World of Libraries

Libraries have not settled on how they define tweens, and generally they take cues from the world of education. Many of the challenges taking place within the school arena are similar for libraries. However, librarians write more about what they do that works. Keep in mind that each community does not define tweens in the same way. Thus, the correlation for successful activities may not be exactly the same. Taking time to look at what the library world is starting to discover about tweens will further develop the overall picture of tweens.

In an article by Crystal Faris, "Betwixt and Between: Tweens in the Library," there is great reliance on information from the world of marketing. She does suggest that both publishers and the library field are beginning to look at defining who tweens are. "Asking questions of tweens, observing their use of the library, and participating in formal research studies all have importance in understanding the population and providing excellent library service" (Faris, 2009). This recommendation lends itself to the idea of tween advisory boards (which will be discussed further in chapter 21) and other formal ways of getting input from tweens.

Looking at library programming for tweens, Amanda Moss Struckmeyer discusses not only examples of successful tween programming but also the importance of tween programming in the library. She also mentions the concept of a continuum of programming for library patrons as well as the long-term benefit that can accrue many years in the future: "A patron who has been attending programs consistently from infanthood through adulthood may engage in more of our library services than a patron who attended storytimes as a toddler but found no appropriate library programming during elementary or middle school" (Struckmeyer, 2012). Realizing the importance of an investment in tweens that will pay off in loyal adult library users is not mentioned in many other articles about tweens. (The continuum of library services will be discussed and expanded further in chapters 17 and 18.)

Public Libraries has published an article by Sarah Bean Thompson about tweens in the library. Some of the ideas are very similar to those from the Struckmeyer article. The importance of either having a tween advisory board or talking with tweens to get ideas for programming is worth repeating. The other point that Thompson's article brings up is the idea of transportation. Tweens may really want to attend a program, but they are dependent on the adults in their life to get them to the library (Thompson, 2013). Visiting schools in order to engage tweens has also been suggested in different library articles, including Thompson's. Whether it is holding a book club there or simply talking to tweens, collaborating with the schools can be very helpful.

While not about a library or tweens in the United States, the TioTretton library in Sweden does provide points to consider when offering library services to tweens. While this special library where only tweens are allowed is designed to be a creative space for tweens, everything is organized to come back to reading. Adults are there to facilitate and ask questions. They are sometimes anti-authority figures or use their lack of knowledge about a particular subject area to engage tweens in conversations (Bayliss, 2013). The emphasis that the administrators of the Stockholm Library put on developing a space to encourage creativity, independence, and reading gives librarians in the United States other ideas regarding ways to think about their spaces and programs for tweens.

A final article from the world of libraries comes from *School Library Journal*, which features interviews conducted with a handful of librarians from around the country who are working specifically with tweens. Many of the topics discussed are common to most library-based articles about tweens, including giving tweens a safe place to be themselves, whether it is creative, nerdy, book loving, or loud. This particular emphasis shows how libraries have discovered the importance of making tweens a valued part of the public library, even though doing that takes more different elements than other groups in the library require. The other point this article brings up is talking to tweens themselves about what they are interested in and what pop culture has the most influence on their lives (Witteveen, 2015). This is a slightly different approach from other articles, but paying attention to pop culture interests in a particular community has much value for librarians.

Looking at the different articles about tweens in libraries, several common themes stand out. There is a focus on having or developing a space just for tweens to be creative, to explore, or simply to be themselves. Programming ideas focus on activities that are creative and interactive. The opportunity to interact with other tweens in the library, either bringing friends to the library with them or meeting people there, shows the vital role of socializing. The need to be independent is also a major priority with tweens, so giving them choices or allowing them to participate in meaningful ways to shape their space or activities is important. Finally, talking to tweens to get ideas is crucial. Tweens are influenced by, and extremely aware of, pop culture. Librarians can learn from tweens and apply that knowledge to developing programs and activities to appeal to the tween population in their community.

The World of Marketing

A majority of the information that is known about tweens comes from research and investigation done by marketers. They were really the first to define tweens as a specific market of consumers to appeal and advertise to. As a result, they have generated potentially the most well-defined picture of who tweens are. However, it is in their best interests to do so in order to capitalize on tweens' buying power. Several articles mention the lack of quantity and quality of information on tweens as a group when compared to other groups. Regardless, marketing still provides the greatest amount of information.

Marketers have been doing research for a while, and Diane Prince and Nora Martin provide a literature review of relevant studies on marketing to tweens. Much of the research is done in other countries, but, regardless of the geography, there seem to be certain conclusions that can be drawn. One area of interest is discovering that marketers still struggle with defining what tweens are (Prince and Martin, 2012). Intellectual and emotional development can range so widely in the tween years that it is difficult to develop a marketing strategy that lasts. Prince and Martin's research finds that tweens do have an influence on what their families purchase. Since tweens are media savvy, they must be marketed to more carefully and specifically. These ideas will resonate with librarians because their challenges are similar to those mentioned in this article.

While *Bloomberg Business* is not strictly a marketing publication, one of its articles on marketing to tweens brings a few more ideas to light. This article mentions that tweens are very brand conscious and critical of advertising techniques; additionally, it calls attention to the fact that there are enough tweens creating a distinct break from childhood that they want products and services of their own (de Mesa, 2005). This reinforces the idea that while tweens are striving for independence, they are still very dependent on their parents for money. As a result, their parents try to exert some control over how tweens spend their money. Also, talking about tween specific brands that have developed to serve this population is a reminder of tween power. Librarians see tweens trying to follow what is popular and their parents trying to maintain some kind of control over what is going on. This can be reflected most in the fact that you may have great ideas for tween programs, especially those generated by the tweens themselves, but if the parents are not interested, the tweens will not be attending.

Another article in *Adweek* goes even further into how connected tweens are on social media. This is all they have ever known, and marketers understand that and work from that place. Tweens "might not yet own devices themselves, but [they] have had parents passing the smartphone or tablet to them in the backseat since they were old enough to hold it" (Goldman, 2012). That is an extremely powerful realization. Computers and other similar devices are an extension of tweens. Marketers must be aware of Internet safety laws for children, but filling their campaigns with interactive and creative online environments is desirable to get tweens' attention. Marketing items that appeal to tweens' need to have an impact on their environment in a way that they find amusing is mentioned several times. Again, the idea that marketers must keep an eye on advertising to tweens' parents is important. Marketers must find a happy medium in successfully reaching out to tweens and their parents. Taking these ideas to the library world, tweens are immersed in technology. That does not necessarily mean having all the latest tech toys, but if the technology is used in meaningful and creative ways, then tweens will be interested. Tweens want to make an impact with what they do, and libraries can offer those types of opportunities. Of course, whatever the parents find important or worthwhile must be part of the attractive package that tween programming or services are wrapped in.

Analyzing tweens' abilities to discern different marketing techniques highlights the developmental milestones that tweens achieve during this period. The *Journal of Advertising Research* has an article about marketing techniques that are less overt—for example, relying on recommendations of "friends" when in fact the friends are being given free products in exchange for product promotion (Freeman and Shapiro, 2014). As tweens mature and are able to identify and label more subtle advertising techniques, they become more jaded and critical of overtly promotional messages. However, that is something that appears to be more directly related to age and cognitive development than anything else. There is a real question as to whether it is right for advertisers to use methods that tweens may not perceive as advertising because of their age and development. Regardless, as soon as tweens identify advertising as such, they have a tendency to develop negative thoughts about the company or product thus advertised. For librarians, this article supports the idea of using tween advisory boards or asking groups of tweens what they like. This information will then attract other tweens who are interested in the same things. However, it also points to the need for libraries to identify who the leaders are within their tween populations and the importance of getting their support and input for programs, materials, or anything that the library would like to market to tweens.

The Atlantic has published an article about what tween television shows actually teach tweens. While not strictly a marketing article, it does point to some important ideas about how tweens behave. There appears to be a fine line in their behavior between wanting to be independent and beginning to rebel against their family or whatever conformity they view as being "just like everyone else." The article fits with several others that address the importance of socializing and the influence that peers have on tweens. It also suggests that tween television is pushing the idea of conformity as a way to survive this turbulent developmental time. Several times the messages of conformity come up with regard to currently popular programs on Disney and Nickelodeon. "Even as they seem to glorify the rogue and untapped energies of youth, [sitcoms] are really tutorials on how to keep those energies within the iron laws of normality—on how to be special but not too special" (Parker, 2015). It seems to be a conflicting message that tweens are both getting and giving: sometimes conformity is desirable, and other times creativity and individuality. Presenting an article that focuses on conformity provides an interesting counterbalance to the articles that emphasize tweens' need to be individuals. For librarians, this is a reminder that there is no "one size fits all" plan for working with tweens. It is necessary to find a balance of offerings.

Following a study of several types of tweens that was conducted to assess the relationship between immersion in the ideas spread by popular culture and their potential for positive life outcomes in some ways at first appears irrelevant. However, it is an interesting study because it openly acknowledges that the research must be expanded to get more reliable data. The study's authors understand that their samples are not as diverse as they would like, and tweens are a very diverse group of individuals. However, what is most interesting is that tweens who are absorbing the most popular culture information tend to be less happy with themselves than tweens who are less invested in popular culture (Scott Comulada, Rotheram-Borus, Carey, Poris, Lord, and Mayfield Arnold, 2011). This development means that tweens, as has been stated before, need a lot of support as they explore who they will become. The potential for tweens to make poor choices when they do not have positive self-esteem is discussed and examined within this article as well. Because of the potential for low self-esteem, the importance of positive peer and adult relationships is mentioned as a way to give tweens a better image of themselves. For librarians, it can be extrapolated from this article that tweens need support, understanding, and openness. This group can be so mercurial that providing consistent support and a welcoming environment may be exactly what some tweens in the community need.

While vastly more academic in nature, "Threshold Lives" points to the idea that even though there is much research available, from the fields of both marketing and child development, it is still very difficult to find exactly the point at which children become teens. This again labels the tween years as those in which there is no consistent or pervasive behavior to allow the development of reliable marketing strategies. While this is not new information, the idea that tweens are interested in and privately practicing strategies and behaviors that they have seen and plan to use when they are older is a new piece to add to the picture (Cody, Lawlor, and Maclaran, 2010). This article comments on the comparative lack of information on tweens, but it follows with other similar articles' findings about this group. It also highlights the great change and inability to conform to one label that characterizes tweens. For librarians, the idea of tweens testing different versions of themselves could sound quite correct and in line with what they observe in the library. Some tweens find the library a safe place to be themselves or be someone other than who they are at home or school, so, as librarians, it is necessary to provide a safe space for experimentation.

An article specifically breaking down techniques for marketing to tweens has many implications for libraries because they must market to tweens as well. Again, the ideas of brand loyalty and being savvy about whether marketers are talking down to them or encouraging them are critical ("Marketing to Tweens," 2008). Tweens will ignore brands that do not appeal to their independence and social nature. If it appears too babyish, they will ignore it. There is some discussion about different products for different genders, and it is possible that marketing those things in distinct ways is necessary. However, this article's tips about understanding that tweens are growing up in a world where computers, the Internet, and even social media have existed for their entire lives makes it helpful for many different groups. Librarians reading this can find some concrete ideas to follow for marketing programs, materials, and services to tweens. However, tweens will be able to tell immediately if the librarian is disingenuous or does not completely believe in what he or she is saying. Thus, it may be best to have multiple staff members work with tweens, assuming each person can effectively market a different part of the library's tween offerings.

Looking at the various marketing articles about tweens, as with the articles from other realms, there are once again common themes. Awareness of pop culture is huge for tweens, but that can have both positive and negative influences. The social aspects are equally important. What peers think, say, do, and recommend is of great importance, but if that is used by marketers without tweens being aware that it is marketing, then there can be problems. There can also be backlashes and negative feelings about brands and companies that appear to overtly market to tweens or are caught by tweens as being disingenuous. Tweens want both individuality and conformity. They want independence, and their parents want control. Tweens want to interact with their marketing and be entertained and engaged. And, most important, they want to be recognized as not a child and not quite yet a teenager. They are different and want to be treated as such.

The Takeaway

Looking at the information gained from the areas of education, libraries, and marketing, it becomes clear that a tween is a mass of contradictions and difficult to define for any length of time. The review of different articles shows that this period of time currently called the tween years is filled with many changes. One tween will be very different from another.

They are developing their abilities to discern the world around them, and yet they sometimes do not. They are mature and immature at the same time. They want conformity and individuality. They are social creatures both online and in person. They want and need adults in their lives who respect them and appreciate their unique gifts and talents. Tweens can also tell when the adults around them are not treating them with respect.

In general, a tween is:

- a male or female between the ages of 9 and 14;
- changing from childlike to adult-like behavior constantly;
- able to function well when clear, consistent boundaries for activities and behaviors are set;
- best able to connect with authority figures who demonstrate respect;
- someone who enjoys and thrives on creative activities;
- looking for activities and experiences to be interactive;
- seeking a safe place to be himself or herself without being judged;
- eager to make a positive or noticeable impact on his or her environment;
- very aware of pop culture, which has both positive and negative affects;

- cognizant of what peers think of him or her;
- desirous of having the approval of peers;
- learning to recognize marketing strategies;
- developing brand loyalty or brand revulsion;
- testing different personality traits and aspects to see what fits him or her best;
- trying to become independent from his or her parents while they still exert some control and influence;
- expecting media to be engaging and interactive;
- more mature than a child but not yet a teenager; and
- exerting enough buying power that companies are marketing products and services to tweens and their parents much more than they did only a short time ago.

REFERENCES

Bayliss, S. (2013). Over 13 not admitted. *Library Journal*, 11.

Cody, K., Lawlor, K., and Maclaran, P. (2010). Threshold lives: Exploring the liminal consumption of tweens. *Advances in Consumer Research*, 17, 346–351.

de Mesa, A. (2005, October 11). Marketing and tweens. *Bloomberg Business.* Retrieved from http://www.bloomberg.com/bw/stories/2005–10-11/marketing-and-tweens

Faris, C. (2009). Betwixt and between: Tweens in the library. *Children & Libraries: The Journal of the Association for Library Service to Children*, 7 (1), 43–45.

Freeman, D., and Shapiro, S. (2014). Tweens' knowledge of marketing tactics: Skeptical beyond their years. *Journal of Advertising Research*, 54 (1), 44–55. doi:10.2501/JAR-54–1-044–055

Goldman, S.M. (2012, June 24). The social tween. *Adweek.* Retrieved from http://www.adweek.com/sa-article/social-tween-141314.

Marketing to tweens: Data, spending habits + dos & don'ts to reach this fickle age group. (2008, June 19). *MarketingSherpa.* Retrieved from https://www.marketingsherpa.com/article/how-to/data-spending-habits-dos-donts.

Marshall, R.M., and Neuman, S. (2012). Brain changes from tween to teen. *Principal*, 44.

Meyers, E. M. (2010). Cognitive authority in everyday life: From small worlds to virtual worlds. *Knowledge Quest*, 38 (3), 48–51.

Morgan, B., and Odom, D. (2006). Stories from tween classrooms. *Educational Leadership*, 63 (7), 38–41.

Parker, J. (2015). What tween TV teaches our kids: The insidious message of Nickelodeon and Disney. *The Atlantic*, 36.

Prince, D., and Martin, N. (2012). The tween consumer marketing model: Significant variables and recommended research hypotheses. *Academy of Marketing Studies Journal*, 16 (2), 31–45.

Scott Comulada, W., Rotheram-Borus, M.J., Carey, G., Poris, M., Lord, L.R., and Mayfield Arnold, E. (2011). Adjustment of trendy, gaming and less assimilated tweens in the United States. *Vulnerable Children & Youth Studies*, 6 (3), 263–275. doi:10.1080/17450128.2011.59779

Struckmeyer, A.M. (2012). Reaching tweens. *Children & Libraries: The Journal of the Association for Library Service to Children*, 10 (2), 36–38.

Thompson, S.B. (2013). Don't forget the tweens. *Public Libraries* (6), 29.

Witteveen, A. (2015). What do tweens want? Librarians create special spaces and services for preteens. *School Library Journal* (10), 30.

Wormeli, R. (2006). Differentiating for tweens. *Educational Leadership*, 63 (7), 14–19.

3

Tween Archetypes

Continuing to develop the picture of a tween, it is time to meld the information from educational and developmental psychology with that of existing writing. This chapter brings the theoretical into a more concrete framework of tweens seen in a library and how these tweens can be helped in library environments.

Both research areas agree that a tween could be as young as eight and as old as fifteen. In order to accommodate the most people, this book uses the age range of 9 to 14. During this period of time, tweens go through tremendous physical, intellectual, experiential, and emotional growth. Tweens push to become independent from their parents, and during this time of growing independence, they are trying new activities and hobbies to find what they like. They are particularly interested in creative activities. Tweens are also extremely concerned about how they are perceived by others, especially their peers; as a result, tweens are susceptible to peer pressure. They are influenced by pop culture but reject being the subject of overt marketing, though they expect to have products and services created specifically for them. They are more mature than children and not as mature as teens.

The publication *Parenting School Years* ran an article several years ago called "Field Guide to the Common Tween." The idea was to briefly describe the different types of tweens, like the Pop Queen-Ager, Mean-Ager, Twony Hawk, Squeaky Clean-Ager, Tweenerd, Green-Ager, Unseen-Ager, Late to Wean-Ager, Go Team-Ager, and Dark-Ager (Moore, 2010). However, for librarians, there are a greater variety of archetypes that are not described in this article. Many tween archetypes are slightly simplified, younger descriptions of teenagers. On a regular basis tweens are participating in activities that used to be the province of primarily teenagers. Individual librarians will encounter more archetypes than are listed here, but this is a start. This is tween archetypes, library edition.

Keep in mind that, regardless of the archetype, tweens must be treated with respect. Condescending behavior results in a librarian being immediately labeled as "another clueless adult" and ignored. Sometimes what is perceived as condescension by tweens is unfortunately the adult being harried and stressed, so keep an eye on that. Investing this time will serve adults well in the long run. Also, be aware that tweens have a well-developed "fib detector"—they can tell when adults are being disingenuous.

Common Tween Archetypes

The Reluctant Reader

The reluctant reader is probably one of the most common library tween archetypes. There probably are not more tween reluctant readers than at any other age, though sometimes it seems that way. This type of tween literally shuffles his or her feet across the floor, head down, and mumbles if the parent with him or her lets the tween speak. Sometimes this tween stands behind or off to the side from the parent. Standing there with the reluctant reader and the parent can be an uncomfortable situation if the parent starts berating the tween about his or her reluctance or if the tween starts arguing with the parent about not wanting to read or be in the library. More often than not, it is the adult with the reluctant reader who is making the scene, and sometimes it becomes a bit loud. Generally the reluctant reader is male, but not always. Frequently the adult does all the talking, but if the tween does talk, it is often monosyllabic answers to questions or the ever common "I don't know."

Reading reluctance can also be a matter of circumstance. As children get into the tween years, there are a lot more activities they can be involved in. Sports and other physical activities can take up a lot of tweens' time. Reluctance to read may not always indicate that the tween has trouble reading. It could be a result of being over-scheduled and overtired. However, another subset of reluctant readers are so labeled by the adults in their lives. These reluctant readers are resistant to read either what is required in school or what may be suggested by parents.

There are many types of materials to suggest to reluctant readers depending on what type of reluctant reader they are. If a reluctance to read comes from difficulty reading, then graphic novels are a great genre to suggest. However, some parents will balk at this suggestion and say it is not truly reading. If this happens, suggest humorous books. Oftentimes these tween books have a healthy dose of illustrations, which makes the reading load lighter, but because they have more words than graphic novels, the parents are happy. The other option would be books that can be related to the tweens' hobbies or media interests. It could be sports books for the sports enthusiast, romantic books for the boy-crazy girl, or books of facts, trivia, or directions for the tween interested only in one topic, instead of narratives. As far as media goes, there is a growing body of media tie-in books, including novelizations of movies, game guides for video games, or narratives that fill in missing parts of the plot for a video game or movie series.

The Lives and Breathes Sports Tween

Sports enthusiasts are seen out in public quite frequently, but this archetype is not seen too often in person in the library. This tween usually wears a sports jersey and warm-up pants for every occasion. The jerseys can be from professional, collegiate, high school, or local sports. If the weather requires a sweatshirt or coat, this, too, will have the insignia of a sports team. Sneakers will almost always be worn, or possibly athletic slides, often with white tube socks showing. If it is warm enough, it will be mesh shorts, usually of basketball player length regardless of whether the rest of the ensemble matches basketball. A hat may or may not be worn, but if it is, it will also have a sports team logo emblazoned across it. This attire is basically the same for both genders.

When this type of tween comes into the library, it is usually for something related to sports. It may be a school project that has nothing to do with sports, but if the librarian can find a way to put a sports spin on the topic, that will be good. Book choices for pleasure reading will be sports fiction or a story where athleticism is a central plot point. Pleasure reading could also be nonfiction about sports. Books of statistics and sports trivia are equally popular, or it could be books about professional teams in a specific sport. They will also read biographies of sports stars, although frequently the sports star they look for does not have a biography published yet. Books of techniques that will help the tween improve in his or her chosen sport are popular as well. Keep in mind that, depending on the needs of the tween, the librarian may need to find material outside the tween section in order to satisfy the particular need.

The Programming Tween

Most programming tweens do not have a consistent uniform. However, this is still an easily recognizable archetype. This tween only comes to specific types of programs. More important, this tween makes a big deal of announcing to anyone within hearing distance that he or she does not read. While it may seem odd to announce this loud and proud in a library, it seems to be a common operating procedure. There will, of course, be some programming tweens who very quietly demonstrate that they are not readers. However, these tweens frequently are avid consumers of the library's audiovisual materials and may even provide librarians with suggestions of things to purchase.

Programming tweens come to every program for tweens that is offered, and they are happy to do so. The topic or time of day doesn't matter—they are there. To encourage these tweens to move beyond borrowing solely AV materials, there are a few types of books that may work. Books that are specific to whatever program is occurring can be of interest, since they extend the experience of the program to the tween's home. The other option is media tie-in books that relate to the movies, music, or video games that the tween currently borrows.

The Specific Program Tween

There is a definite subset of the Programming Tween that shares many similarities, like publicly proclaiming not reading, consuming library audiovisual materials, and being devoted attendees to programs. The difference is that it is only a very specific program that attracts such tweens, and as a librarian, there is very little that you can do to change this! This type of tween sometimes is involved in many activities and only has time for one specific program. More frequently, this tween has very narrow interests, and if a library program fits that interest, then the tween attends. Examples of these types of tweens would be ones who only come to video game, board game, crafting, LEGO, or lock-in events, to name a few. Recommending books to Specific Program Tweens follows the same guidelines as for the Programming Tweens. However, these Specific Program Tweens are ones who would be good in a library tween advisory group. They will advocate for and maintain a high standard of quality for the programs that they are interested in. They will also bring like-minded tweens to library programs that librarians could not do on their own.

The Seasonal Tween

Technically this, too, is a subset of the Programming Tween, but the Seasonal Tween tends to be in the library only during a certain time of the year. There are two types of Seasonal Tweens: those who come to the library only during the summer, and others who come only during the school year.

Summer Seasonal Tweens tend to participate in summer reading, both the reading program itself and any other activities at the library during that time. Many of them are avid readers, but not all. They are completely devoted to the library, and they are seen constantly, but only during a specific period of time. During the rest of the calendar year their attentions are elsewhere, or in some cases they live somewhere else, but during the summer they are visiting some relative or staying somewhere that makes your library the one they use.

The school year Seasonal Tweens are seen on a regular basis. They tend to be both readers and attenders of programs, although they probably identify themselves more as readers. They will tell librarians when school lets out for the summer, "See you in the fall," or some equivalent. There can be many different reasons for this summertime absence. Sometimes it has to do with the proximity of the library to their school and the tweens' inability to get transportation to the library during the summer. Another reason for tweens to disappear in the summer can have to do with family plans during the summer that do not include the library, like traveling to another geographic location or being farmed out to other family members due to custodial arrangements.

Since generally these Seasonal Tweens are readers, book recommendations would be things that have been published since the last time they were in the library. For the school year Seasonal Tweens, it would be books that came out during the summer, and for the summer Seasonal Tweens, ones that have come out since the previous summer. It can be difficult, but these tweens would also be good on the library's tween advisory board. They will advocate for programs and activities during the time that they use the library.

The Off-Season Tween

The Off-Season Tween is related to the Lives and Breathes Sports Tween as well as the Seasonal Tween. However, this is a tween who is seen only between sports seasons (or other types of activities). This means it could only be a handful of weeks at a time a few times a year. Although sports are the focus for the majority of this archetype, tweens participating in the drama club, for example, can also present as an Off-Season Tween. This tween usually dresses like a Lives and Breathes Sports Tween, with jerseys, warm-up pants, sneakers, and the like. Whatever the activity is that takes up most of the tweens' time, there is probably some type of clothing item advertising that activity.

The Off-Season Tween will be present in the library for programs or to simply use the library when his or her activity is over for the season or on hiatus for a period of time. These tweens will voraciously consume library services, reading many materials and attending many programs during their "off time." It's feast or famine with these tweens. They will be seen every day for a week or two, and then not again for three months.

Librarians can provide these tweens with substantial service. They will probably want to talk quite a bit during the brief days they are in the library. They will want not only to share what they have been doing for the past few months but also to catch up on the events of the library. The librarian's greatest impact on these tweens will be making sure they know about the new and popular books that have come out during the time they were busy. These tweens will also be looking for fun, quick, light reads to fill in their temporarily empty blocks of time.

The Reading Tween

This type of tween will present as the more traditional library-loving tween. He or she will probably evince one or two popular librarian stereotypes, such as wearing glasses, ignoring popular fashion trends, or being socially awkward. However, do not assume that all Reading Tweens look this way. More often than not, there are no distinguishing clothing or behavioral features to help identify a Reading Tween, except perhaps a T-shirt for a favorite book or book series that has become a movie. Reading Tweens are probably giving librarians book suggestions, particularly if their specific interest is not well represented in the tween collection. A Reading Tween may also not be reading exclusively in the tween fiction collection. He or she may be delving into the materials in youth nonfiction or in the young adult area—possibly even in the adult fiction or nonfiction collections, depending on the area of interest, reading level, and parental permissions.

Reading tends to be the Reading Tweens' sole hobby and passion. They frequently do not attend tween programs. For whatever reason, this is not their thing. There can be many different reasons for this, ranging from being shy to program times not fitting tweens' schedules or general disinterest in programming topics. As a librarian, do whatever is necessary to find appropriate books for the Reading Tweens, including asking for help from colleagues whose areas of expertise better match what these tweens are looking for. However, these tweens will probably not ask for many book recommendations, as they are voracious readers or devotees of a particular genre or author. However, these tweens are good potential tween advisory group members. This could be a hard sell because they often do not participate in programs. But if they do become part of the group, they will be advocates for the tween collection or the overall library collection, especially as it relates to their area of interest. And if their suggestions of materials do not correspond to the tween area, they can be forwarded to the appropriate collection development person at the library. Following up with both the staff person and the tween so that the material is ordered and the tween knows that his or her suggestion is valued gives the library increased credibility with tweens.

The Child Care Tween

These tweens can seem like Programming Tweens or Reading Tweens on the surface, but, looking deeper, they are slightly different. These tweens are in the library all the time. They do not have a particular uniform or look about them, but they are always around.

There can be two very closely related types of Child Care Tweens. One you see only if your library is located near a school; they are some of the first through the library door after school, and they stay until far into the evening. They will happily participate in whatever programs occur after school. They probably have some favorite authors or genres. They can be found curled up in a corner for hours reading. They will also spend long periods of time using library computers or using their own devices with the library's Wi-Fi connection. However, you will probably not see them during the summer or on the weekends. They come because their parents have told them to go to the library after school. Occasionally, if you get a large number of these tweens all together, there can be some behavioral issues due to "groupthink." Individually these tweens are great, and they love the library and its services. However, get too many Child Care Tweens in the same place, and they can become boisterous or choose to participate in activities they think up themselves that may not be the best ones to carry out in the library at that time.

The other type of Child Care Tween is the one who is dropped off early for programs and picked up late. Like the other type, these tweens love coming to library programs, and they probably have favorite authors or genres as well. However, they are aware, if only on a subconscious level, that their parents left them to go do something else. For younger tweens, this can be a problem when their parents don't pick them up on time. They can feel abandoned and unimportant. Additionally, depending on where they are in their emotional development, this can lead to crying and real angst on the tween's part.

However, there are some ways to make Child Care Tweens feel important to the library. Most likely they don't need material recommendations; they probably already have a stack of books to check out each time they visit, and they are already attending almost every program available. However, they will be more than willing to help around the library if asked. Sometimes they will ask a librarian if there is anything they can do to help. This help can come in a variety of forms. They can be asked to be part of the tween advisory board, particularly if it meets while they are already there waiting to get picked up. Depending on how the library is set up, unionized or not, Child Care Tweens could help around the tween area of the library or even in the children's area. They can always help clean up after programs. If there are events for other age groups, like young children, to prepare for, is there something tweens can do, like set-up a craft or get out materials for an activity? Tweens can also pick up books in the tween area that need to be shelved and set them aside to be put away later. They can straighten the shelves in the tween area so bookends are straight and displays are appealing and organized. Giving the tweens an opportunity to help in their section gives them a sense of ownership. Things get cleaned up, and the librarian does not have to do it! Some tweens will be more than happy to do the same types of cleaning and straightening up in the children's area. They like to be the big person helping little kids, even if they are only a year or two older than the children in that area! Depending on the library's policies on volunteers, if there are tweens at the library quite regularly, they can be assigned library volunteers with very specific tasks expected of them. The idea is to make the most of what could be a tricky situation with this archetype.

Summer Child Care Tween

The Summer Child Care Tween in some ways is related to the Child Care Tween, but in other ways they are totally different. Summer Child Care tweens usually are not seen during the school year, but in some instances Child Care Tweens can become Summer Child Care Tweens. These tweens can be at the library regardless of where the library is located in relation to any other places tweens can be found. They are sent to the library because their parents have somewhere they must be during the summer (usually work). These tweens are dropped off at the library, usually by a parent, fairly early in the morning and not picked up until dinnertime or later. These tweens can be identified in several ways. Frequently they are waiting outside the door to the library before it opens in the morning. Sometimes they are dropped off just at opening time. Sometimes these tweens are here from the moment the library opens until the moment it closes. These tweens usually have a backpack or bag of some kind with whatever supplies they will need for the day. (Ideally one of the supplies is food for the tween to eat during the day or money for vending machines, if such things exist at the library.) Usually they have a library card of their own to check out books, and more often now they have a smartphone or some type of device with which to entertain themselves. More often than not they are capable of entertaining themselves for some portion of the day; the challenge is when they get bored, since they will find other things to do. If there are too many Summer Child Care Tweens in the library, then the behavior challenges of Child Care Tweens present themselves. However, the options for creating positive interactions with Child Care Tweens are also the same strategies to use with Summer Child Care Tweens. If there is a way to make the Summer Child Care Tweens feel important and a part of the library, that goes a long way toward curtailing behavior problems and making these tweens feel special.

The Displaced Tween

These tweens are a very specific subset of Child Care Tweens and generally only seen at libraries that are located within walking distance of schools. While that is not always the case, this archetype is probably the most community-dependent type of tween. Some places will have these, and some will not. What makes these tweens different from Child Care Tweens is that Displaced Tweens do not want to be at the library. They are there because there is nowhere else for them to go. Sometimes the tweens are in the library because they have "aged out" of formal child care within the community. They could be viewed by their parents as too young to be home alone for several hours, so the parents tell them to go to the library. They could also be marking time at the library before another activity starts at the school or some other nearby location. There isn't enough time to go home after school and come back, or there is no way to get back to the school or other location after getting home. Generally, Displaced Tweens do not have library cards or participate in library programs, even if the program is occurring while they are in the building. They are at the library because they have to be, and so their regard for the social mores of the library may be minimal. It does not take many of these tweens to create behavior problems, and unfortunately it can be this specific archetype of tweens that give the whole group a bad name in the eyes of other library staff, patrons, or community members.

However, it is with this group of tweens specifically that it is necessary to remember how tweens develop. Some of the behaviors that are perfectly normal for them are those that may drive librarians absolutely crazy. Displaced Tweens are highly susceptible to groupthink, and succumbing to peer pressure is quite common at this age. For example, groupthink can mean that one tween decides that the group should play hide and seek in the stacks while they wait to go back to the school for play practice, and the rest go along with this proposal. When groupthink is at work, logical thinking is suspended. What one tween knows to be a bad idea sounds, in a group, like a great idea. Displaced Tweens also display childlike behaviors. This can be pushing, shoving, hitting, and taking something that does not belong to them. Behaviors normally associated with toddlers or preschoolers can be on full display with a group of Displaced Tweens. However, remember that this seemingly childlike behavior is really about performing for a group. Tweens believe that everyone is watching them, and when they do something childish, people are paying attention. Negative versus positive attention does not always matter to them. Someone is watching them and reacting to what they are doing, and that is most important. Related to the idea that everyone is watching them is when small groups of tweens "parade" around the library or wherever they are able to roam. They sit down for a few minutes, walk in a set pattern around whatever space they have, and then sit down again. This is done repeatedly. They want other tweens to notice them as they are walking around the library.

Having a successful relationship with Displaced Tweens is not as straightforward as it is for other archetypes. However, it is not impossible. The first thing to keep in mind is that no matter how frustrating they were yesterday, today is a new day. They must be greeted just as warmly as anyone else. However, if one or more Displaced Tweens do not follow the library's rules of behavior, librarians must calmly and consistently follow the procedures to correct or end the behavior. Consistency is key when dealing with large groups of Displaced Tweens. This group may also provide a readymade opportunity to collaborate with outside groups within the community. There may be ways to give the Displaced Tweens somewhere to go or something to do that allows them to have a positive experience either in the library or somewhere else. If there are smaller numbers of Displaced Tweens, they may be used to advantage. Can they share with adults what is popular and provide a different perspective to the tween advisory board? Are they willing to clean up parts of the library is exchange for a snack? (Displaced Tweens are frequently hungry, and they will behave much better after being fed.) How else can this challenging group of tweens become an asset for the library?

The Busy Tween

These tweens are readers. They do not read as much as the Reading Tweens because they are doing a wide variety of other activities, but they do read. They tend to be school and community spirit–minded individuals. While they may play sports, they are not solely focused on sports. They may be musicians, actors, student council members, or Scouts, to name a few common tween activities. Busy Tweens have favorite authors and genres, and they tend to favor putting books on hold because then they simply come to the library when what they want is available. There is no distinct physical look to these tweens, but many dress in the current fashions of the season. They tend to be well dressed and well groomed.

They do not attend tween programs, or if they do, it is one or two a year. They have so much going on that frequently the timing of programs conflicts with something else they are doing. There probably aren't too many books that can be recommended to Busy Tweens. They usually do not come to the library to browse but to pick up holds or grab something very quickly between activities. However, if asked, these tweens will usually try to make time for tween advisory groups, and it is worth inviting them. Some Busy Tweens are also part of influential peer groups that can attract new tweens to the library. In addition, these tweens tend to have a solid handle on pop culture and what is popular in their community. This can be valuable information to have.

The Outreach Tween

Outreach Tweens are never seen in the library. There are no uniforms or general physical characteristics for this group. However, they are seen during community programming. There are two types of Outreach Tweens. First, there are some whose families, for whatever reason, will not come to the library. There can be several fairly common explanations for this. One reason can be the tweens' parents had a bad experience with a library or a specific librarian in their past. Frequently the bad experience had absolutely nothing to do with the library their tween is affiliated with. Another common reason is the parents have numerous fines on their cards, and if they or their children come to the library, they will have to deal with that problem. Another reason is the parents do not want to be responsible for their tweens checking out library materials either because they feel their tweens are careless or because they simply do not want one more thing to be responsible for.

The second type of Outreach Tween is the one whose family is super busy. The difference between this type of Outreach Tween and a Busy Tween is that the Outreach Tween does not come to the library at all, whereas a Busy Tween somehow fits it into their schedule. This second type of Outreach Tween may have parents whose work hours do not mesh with the times the library is open. This could also be a tween from a large family where there are so many people and so many activities that it is hard to get to the library. An Outreach Tween may also be one who has parents who need to be working all the time, so that there is just no time in the week to get to the library.

However, despite the obstacles that Outreach Tweens face, they are usually the most grateful to see library staff when they visit wherever the tweens are. It could be that Outreach Tweens are seen when visiting the local schools, afterschool care facilities, or summer day camps. These tweens will look forward to the library visits and remember and talk about them long after they are done. However, unless the library has a way for these tweens to check out its materials, recommending books to them is not going to be successful. Outreach Tweens usually want to be at the library reading or participating in activities. As a result, librarians working with this group need to show some extra compassion and sensitivity. They must walk a fine line between promoting library services and materials and not making the Outreach Tweens feel excluded or inferior because they cannot do and get what everyone else can based on decisions their parents have made on their behalf. Some libraries are beginning to offer library cards with very limited borrowing privileges, where the library itself assumes the financial responsibility of lost or damaged materials. Outreach Tweens will want to read whatever they can get their hands on from the public library if there is a way that they can do so.

The Nostalgic Tween

These tweens are somewhat related to the Outreach Tweens and the Busy Tweens because they have a little bit of each type within them. Nostalgic Tweens were very active in library activities when they were younger. Their parents brought them to baby storytimes and preschool programs. They probably even came to library programs for young elementary schoolers. Mostly likely they took out a lot of books with their parents when they were little. Many probably have their own library cards, but most may not know where they are anymore. Many were memorable small children either because of their regular storytime attendance or because they had a fixation at some point with a particular topic or type of book. Nostalgic Tweens have fond memories of their time at the library, but they no longer come there. These tweens often go out of their way to acknowledge library staff in public. It can be something as simple as "I used to go there when I was little," or "I remember when I came to the library and we did...." If the tweens recognize library workers from their childhood, oftentimes they will call that staff member out to reminisce about a particular experience, beginning with "Do you remember when I came to [fill in the blank] at the library?" Whatever they did at the library, it made quite an impression on them.

There can be different reasons why these tweens no longer come to the library. It can be because their numerous activities do not allow them enough time to come anymore. It can be that their family situation has changed and parents who used to bring them to library activities all the time now work or work at a different time than before. There can be a large portion of Nostalgic Tweens at outreach locations, but they are different from Outreach Tweens because at some point they had a relationship with the library. Nostalgic Tweens may also be unaware of all that is going on at the library. There could have been a time in their past when the books they wanted were not available or the current slate of programs was uninteresting, so they extrapolated that the library was no longer for them. They outgrew it.

Regardless of what type of Nostalgic Tweens exist around the library, telling them about the new materials, programs, and services available for tweens may help them decide to come back. With this type of tween, listening is particularly important. Hearing what they really enjoyed at the library as a child, and their explanation of why they no longer come to the library, can be quite helpful. If it seems like they are providing an opening to talk about new things going on the library, then do that. If that does not seem like a possibility, then the best thing to do is to tell them, "I'm so glad you enjoyed the library when you were little. If you ever decide to come back to the library, I hope you come and find me. I'd love to see you and show you all the new things we have going on here." That tween needs to continue to have great memories and thoughts about the library.

The Milk and Cookies Tween

This is a special breed of tweens, and they will be one of the last archetypes identified within the community because from the outset they may present like a variety of other archetypes. However, members of this group do tend to have a somewhat similar look and behavior. These tweens may have some hygiene issues not immediately evident. They may need to bathe more, or their clothes may need stronger detergents and more frequent washings. Their clothes may also seem inappropriate for the season outside. This is not to say that all Milk and Cookies Tweens are of a lower socioeconomic class—they are not. Collectively they are much more oblivious to pop culture and the social norms around them than most tweens. Many of them are single minded in their pursuits of hobbies or interests, with little regard for what their peers think of what they are doing. They do, however, want adults to appreciate what it is that they are doing.

These are the tweens who come to mind when reading about Maslow's hierarchy of needs. These children fluctuate between the third and fourth stages of that hierarchy, trying to satisfy their needs for belonging and respect. It can be a very fine line for tweens who both want to be accepted and want to be respected for who they are. This group is called the Milk and Cookies Tweens because they want an adult to listen to them while they talk. They evoke the quintessential 1950s perfect family scenario where the stay-at-home mother has warm cookies and a cold glass of milk waiting at the kitchen table when the child comes home from school. Then the mother sits there and listens patiently and attentively while the child talks about what happened at school. The child knows that the snack and the active listening mean that he or she is valued by the adult.

These tweens want the undivided attention of an adult who is paying attention to and caring about what they share. Library colleagues who work with adults may actually identify this archetype sooner because they will see similar behaviors in older adults who live alone and come to the library, where their interaction with library staff and patrons may be the only human contact they have all day. As a result, they may try to talk someone's ear off. In the library, these tweens more often than not are creative. They want someone to read their short story, praise their poem, admire their artwork, or exclaim over their sewing project. They may want someone to try what they baked in school or listen to them practice their lines for the play. They are looking for an adult's feedback, and they are desperately hoping it is positive. If constructive criticism is necessary, present it as gently and supportively as possible. They want an adult's approval. Generally, with this archetype, these tweens are not getting the support and respect in their home life that they want. As a result, they are looking for that validation elsewhere.

These tweens are giving librarians the power to make them confident or doubtful. This is not a responsibility to be taken lightly, but it can be done successfully. There is also a subset of the Milk and Cookie Tweens who want program leaders to admire the tweens' skills in the program. This generally happens during library-sponsored craft or gaming programs. While tweens are making crafts, they call for the adult leading the program to come over and admire their work. During gaming programs, they want the program leader to see how they win the game, how awesome their game cards are, or how skilled they are at a particular maneuver. This is most common in video game programs, but in card-based programs where the tweens bring their own cards that they have collected and organized, those need to be admired by someone!

For these tweens, there are several different ways to engage them further with the library. They can be offered materials that support what they are working on or passionate about. For example, writers can be offered books on how to write in different styles or given examples of quality authors writing the same types of things they are attempting. For the artists and other creative tweens, there will also be instruction books and collections of projects they can attempt to create. Gaming tweens can be pointed toward game guides or media tie-in novels. Librarians can invite some of these tweens to advise them personally or join the tween advisory group so they can use their knowledge of a particular area, like writing or art, to create similar activities that the library can offer for other tweens in the community. Finally, but not necessarily related directly to the library, if there are staff in the building who are interested in art, drama, whatever, and there is a showing or presentation of the tween's work, go as a group to the event. By attending, the tweens seen in the library all the time have the opportunity to show off for the library staff, but by going with a group from work, there is no chance that being at the event could be viewed by anyone as inappropriate because it is a group of colleagues supporting an event in the community. Unfortunately, these days no one can be too careful.

Special Needs Tweens

The special needs archetype has so many variations. There are numerous physical or mental challenges that can garner the label of "special needs" for a tween. This can include having a diagnosis on the autism spectrum, ADHD, a physical impairment, a developmental delay, or a mental health issue. Regardless of what label they may have, Special Needs Tweens deserve as much respect and appreciation as other tweens. Lately when people mention Special Needs Tweens in libraries, it is in reference to tweens on the autism spectrum. However, there can be any number of tweens, labeled and unlabeled, using the library.

Some challenges can be visually identified, and if it is a matter of making sure things are ADA (Americans with Disabilities Act) compliant, then do that. However, many special needs are not visible to the naked eye, though they may be discerned after seeing a tween's behavior. Generally, but not always, parents will let librarians know if they are bringing tweens with special needs to a program. Always be willing to talk with the parents who may be nervous about leaving their tweens to attend the program. Make sure that both the tweens and the parents are comfortable.

However, there is a subset of Special Needs Tweens who are very rarely mentioned. These are people who chronologically are much older than tweens, but developmentally their cognitive and emotional skills are comparable to those of a 9-to-14-year-old. It is the decision of both the tween librarian and the library administration as to whether people will be allowed to attend tween programs solely based on chronological age or if mental age will be taken into consideration. It is best to take a person-by-person/program-by-program approach. Gaming programs seem to be an area where more Special Needs Tweens congregate because practically everyone can play video games. It can be an arena where the playing field is level, when in real life it is not. Tweens with a variety of special needs can compete against or work with tweens not labeled with a special need. Games like Pokémon and Yu-Gi-Oh! have also been venues in which Special Needs Tweens, especially older people who developmentally are at a tween level, have excelled. However, the success of integrating Special Needs Tweens into library programs will depend on the leader of the program setting the tone of acceptance and mutual support. Fortunately, many tweens are already open to integrating anyone, regardless of age, race, or ability, into their activity if that person displays the same level of enthusiasm that the tweens have. However, tweens will look to librarians and their behaviors, and when they see the librarians treating everyone, regardless of label, with respect, then they will too.

To encourage Special Needs Tweens to interact more with the library, suggest materials that support their interests. Look to their parents in case there are things they do or do not want their children reading. These tweens may need materials that are either simpler or more in depth than what is available within the tween collection. Make sure to provide Special Needs Tweens with the same high level of attention and service that is given to other archetypes. Additionally, these tweens may be interested in trying other types of programming. You can always suggest that option to them, but do not be surprised if they are single minded in their focus on one hobby or interest.

The Well-Rounded Tween

This is every librarian's favorite tween archetype. These tweens are voracious readers, and they attend practically every library program. They may have grown up in the library, or they may be a transplant from some other place but now use this library. There are no particular physical characteristics common to these tweens. They may dress in the current style, or they may march to the beat of their own drummer. They may be surrounded by friends, or they may work alone. They frequently come from families that are strong library supporters; in many cases the whole family reads and comes to the library together. These are the tweens who believe that the library is their second home. They take pride in the building, its materials, and the programs provided. They may be interested in hearing about the newest book to recommend, but they may have their own ideas to follow. They probably are the bedrocks of the tween advisory board, and if they are not, they should be. They are lovers of traditional library services as well as curious about potential new offerings. They are library cheerleaders in the community with their peers and within the library building. These are the people whose support you want when you try something new, including creating a separate tween space within the library. These tweens sometimes function as the gatekeepers to the other tweens in the community. This is not to say that if the Well-Rounded Tweens don't support a program or service, you shouldn't do it, but it is worthwhile testing it out with these very loyal tween patrons and evaluating their feedback. Every librarian would love a large group of Well-Rounded Tweens in their library.

The Takeaway

As stated earlier in this chapter, there are many different tween archetypes; some of those listed above may not match the community in which you live, and some from your community may not be listed here. Remember, there is no reliable and successful way to label tweens. They are too changeable at this period in their lives.

Regardless of whether the majority of the tweens in the library are Displaced Tweens, Specific Program Tweens, or Reading Tweens, everyone is treated the same. Tweens need:

- clear, consistent boundaries;
- respect;
- patience;
- to feel valued;
- options for expressing themselves creatively;
- opportunities for personal growth;
- materials supporting a variety of interests;
- quality reference and reader's advisory services;
- opportunities to share their knowledge with their peers and adults;
- opportunities to make a meaningful impact on their library; and
- adults who treat them each day like it is a new day, giving tweens the opportunity to be the best versions of themselves instead of being condemned by their past mistakes.

REFERENCES
Moore, F. (2010). Field guide to the common tween. *Parenting School Years, 24* (6), 100–103.

4

Tweens in Your Community

Now it is time to look beyond library walls to see what individual communities say about who tweens are. The age span may not be correct the first time—after all, tweens are a moving target. But over time librarians will figure out which are the determining factors that the community needs to consider. The real question is this: Where in the community will information on tweens come from?

What about the Research on Tweens or the Marketing Materials?

The concept of who a tween is will be unique to each community. Research is wonderful and provides a good foundation for understanding youth development, but it will not help with the basic challenges being faced. In the end, tweens are who their community makes them.

Marketing and advertising experts have an idea of who a tween is, but that may not fit perfectly in a particular community. How close is a shopping center? How affluent is the community? The difference between the closest mall being five or twenty-five minutes away will impact how easily a community's tweens can get the "must-have" clothing item or newest version of the iPhone. Or the distance may not be in miles but in money. If it is mostly middle-class families in the community, how easy is it for them to upgrade their cell phone each time Apple brings out a new model? Will they buy the newest game console as soon as it comes out or wait until stores have refurbished models available? Material possessions can sometimes define who in your community is a tween.

For example, in one community it seemed that a child was considered a tween when, in the eyes of their parents, he or she could take care of and use an iPod Touch. This seemed to happen around third or fourth grade, and it was almost always a refurbished iPod Touch purchased online. In another community, a tween was defined as someone responsible enough to have a cell phone. However, this is only one factor to consider.

How Are the Schools Organized?

Another place to look for some clues as to who tweens might be are the schools that the library serves. How many elementary schools are there? What grades are included? Are all the schools organized in the same way, or do different school districts group children differently in the buildings? Is there a junior high or a middle school?

There are lots of different ways in which schools can be organized. For example, if the local schools are organized such that fifth through eighth graders are grouped in the same building, then that might be your tween age range right there. However, some communities have schools that subdivide kindergarten through second grade in one building, third through fifth in another, and sixth through eighth grade in a third building. More commonly, elementary school is kindergarten through fifth or sixth grade. Of course, in certain communities there can be private schools or parochial schools that have kindergarten through eighth grade all in one building. There are even more grade-level organizational schemes beyond these few. Every community is different.

The other thing to consider about schools is majority rules. If the library covers many school districts and each district groups children differently, where do a majority of regular library users go to school? If there is not a consistent answer, there must be some other pattern regarding who comes to the library and where they attend school.

How Do Different Entities in the Community Group Children?

Each community has a different focus. Some are big into sports. Other communities have a strong arts presence. There may be some very influential religious institutions there. What is important in the community? The following are some suggestions but by no means an exhaustive list.

In some places, Boy Scouts and Girl Scouts are important. Here are a few things to keep in mind: The highest level in Cub Scouts, Webelos Scouts, comprises boys from fourth and fifth grade. Boy Scouts begins in fifth or sixth grade, depending on how quickly boys achieve certain goals. For Girl Scouts, Junior Scouts are fourth and fifth graders, and then Cadette Scouts are sixth through eighth graders.

Does the community have a YMCA? Do they use specific age groups for certain types of programs? At what age can children start taking hip hop dance classes? When are children too old for summer camp but can begin as a counselor-in-training for summer camp? What programs they have and who can attend can have a huge impact on what libraries ultimately decide to do in many different areas of tween services.

Section I. Who Is a Tween?

Who teaches art classes and what can be learned when? It could be as simple as when dancers begin wearing pointe shoes in ballet classes at the local art center, or when a person can take a different kind of drama class. What determines when a child becomes more grown-up? A lot of times fourth grade, ages 9–10, is a big divider within fine arts activities.

Church activities can also be important. What age do children begin religion classes, get confirmed, or join social groupings or Bible studies? The age at which most of the youths in a religious community become recognized as adults may be a good guide for determining the upper age range of tweens. Frequently, eighth grade seems to be when youths become full members of their chosen religious denominations.

Sports are probably the biggest factor in helping to determine tween age ranges. At what age do children move between divisions in youth football? When can a child be on a traveling soccer team? What age does cheerleading or twirling start? Can a child be on a traveling basketball team yet? When do the divisions in softball or baseball change? These are all indicators of who is growing up but still not quite old enough for more mature sporting activities.

The influence that community groups have on decisions about who tweens are assumes that librarians have really looked into all the different elements of their communities. Taking time to investigate is well worth it because how those community groups operate will influence other decisions made in different areas of tween service plans. Sometimes community groups are almost more important than the schools (perhaps not in deciding the age of tweens, but more probably in determining when and what programs are ultimately offered).

How Mobile Is the Community?

This was alluded to at the beginning of this chapter when the distance to the mall was mentioned. How often and how far people in the community travel away from home is a bigger factor than one might think in this day and age of connecting through cyberspace. Gasoline can be expensive, after all.

Is the library part of a commuting community? Is it no big deal to drive 30–45 minutes to get to something like a mall, theater, or the downtown portion of a decent-sized city? If parents of prospective tweens think nothing of hopping in the car and driving some distance away to do or see something, their children will have a much wider range of experiences than tweens whose parents don't want to (or can't) travel.

However, if the library is in a metropolitan area or some area with easily accessible public transportation, the story is different in two ways. First, there may be a much wider range of things available to tweens in the metropolitan area than in a rural or suburban area. More important, the age when youths are generally allowed to travel independently might be a determining factor indicating either the beginning or the ending of the tween phase of life.

Beyond automobiles, are there other ways for youths to get around? Is the community bicycle friendly? Are there sidewalks or walking paths? Does the community have a lot of subdivisions with tons of houses in them? How easily can youths gather with their friends without the help of an adult driving a car?

What Is the General Economic State of the Community?

We know that almost every community contains a wide variety of economic levels. There are people who are very wealthy, people who are poor, and plenty of people in between. The question is really where the majority of the community falls on the scale of wealth.

Some believe that the more wealthy a community is, the more "worldly wise" its youths are. They will own more expensive consumer items. They will be involved in more activities and have a much broader sense of the world around them. In communities where there is not as much wealth, youths are less knowledgeable of the world outside. Or, even if they know what is happening "out there," they cannot afford to take part.

However, there is also something to be said for children who have to grow up too fast, and that can be economic as well. In areas of great poverty, youths may have to be responsible for younger siblings at what may seem like a very young age while a parent is at work. A young child may have more household chores to complete because adults are not around. Such youths are much more knowledgeable of the ways of the world, even though they do not have the money to buy consumer items.

How Are Ages Distributed Across the Community?

There are plenty of articles on the Internet discussing how the millennials are going to be as large a generation as the baby boomers. As a result, there will be a lot of children, tweens, and teens moving through the libraries. Check census records or various websites to see what the population distribution is in the library's community. Another place to look is the public schools' projections. Are the districts projected to grow or shrink in the future? And ultimately, exactly how many tweens is the library likely to see?

Kindergarten cut-off birthdays are important to tween services as well. Communities have different dates for when a child has to have turned 5 in order to go to kindergarten. This will make a difference when determining the tween age range. How old are they really when they are in fourth or fifth grade?

How Do the Different Factors Come Together?

It would be great to say there is a magic weighted age formula that is 25 percent school, 50 percent community groups, 10 percent travel, 10 percent money, and 5 percent age distribution, and using this formula will produce the community's perfect tween age range. Sadly, it does not work like that. Every community is different, and the previously mentioned factors will carry different weights. Observing the library's community, talking to parents of regular library-using youths, and exercising some trial and error are truly how any and every library will determine who their tweens are.

When deciding on an age range, how "streetwise" children are will greatly determine how wide the age range needs to be. What is "streetwiseness?" Sadly, it does not appear to be an actual word yet. However, it describes the level of awareness that tweens have. Are they cognizant of different social trends? Whom are they emulating from popular culture? How are they dressing? What technology do they own? How do they behave among their peers? Being aware of popular trends but not following them can be due to the interactions of the factors mentioned before. Tweens may not be able to follow through on these trends or deem them not worth following based on other life factors.

What to Do Next?

Librarians have to keep reevaluating decisions about who is a tween in the community. This group is the most changeable of any in the library. Assuming that only one community evaluation is necessary is dangerous for the long-term health of tween services. It is vital to keep tabs on changes within all the different factors that affect what makes a tween. For example, has a new shopping center opened that is close by? Is there a new community group that has come to prominence? Is there a new sport that every child wants to play? Has the socioeconomic status of the area been raised? How is this changing the buying power of the community in general, and tweens in particular? All of these factors could increase or decrease the age range of the community's tweens.

The Takeaway

Tweens will always be a moving target. Accept this and move on to the next challenge in defining the library's tween services. However, do not be afraid of doing the research in the community and asking questions. In talking to people and finding out more about the community than could possibly be known before, one lays the groundwork for talking to these same people a little later about how beneficial library services for tweens will be.

- Look to how the schools are organized to get a hint as to the grades that tweens may be in.
- Research the community's sports, arts, Scouts, and religious activities to see if there are major divisions that signal a move to more mature levels.
- Community mobility can mean physically whether people walk more or must drive cars everywhere, or it can refer to the economic status of the community, which can change with the overall economic status of the greater municipalities or even the nation as a whole.
- There is no magic weighted formula to use in determining which community factors have more influence regarding who tweens are in the community.

SECTION II

Gathering Support for Tween Services

There is no right way to go about garnering support for tween services in the library. Different readers will need to obtain support from different colleagues and perhaps in a different order than is presented here.

The first chapter in this section deals with getting administrative support for beginning specific tween services in the library. This assumes that the reader is somewhere in the middle of the organizational chart. However, the closer the reader is to the bottom of the chart, the more levels of administration he or she may have to convince in order to get approval to start the new program. However, it is important to get everyone on board with the tween services plan.

The second chapter is written from the perspective of being part of the administration tasked with getting people from lower levels of the organizational chart to become excited about and support tween services. This account should be helpful for administrators, but non-administrators might consider this a way to help convince their own administration of the importance of tween services. It will allow the reader to see the process of developing tween services from a different viewpoint.

The third chapter is about getting colleagues excited about tween services. They may work with other patrons, but it is quite beneficial for them to believe in tween services and understand why they are good for the library. Colleagues are probably the toughest group to convince that tween services are important, depending on what their preconceived ideas about tweens are. However, their support of the project ensures a much better potential success rate.

The final chapter of this section is about getting support from the community. In some ways this is a precursor to community outreach to tweens, but it is really about explaining to people why tweens deserve separate services. This could be especially important if at some point the library needs community support (generally in the form of money) for something relating to tweens.

5

Administrative Support for Tween Services

Obtaining the support of one's administration for a new branch of library services can be tough, and one may need a thick skin if support for tween services does not come immediately and quickly. Also, just because chapters are in a specific order in this book (with the chapter on support from the administration coming before the one detailing support from colleagues), that does not mean that this is the order things must always follow. It may be better in a particular library to get colleagues on board first and then go to administration for support. Some institutions prefer grassroots group ideas better than something generated solely from the administration. Only staff members of a particular library will know in what order to proceed and to whom ideas must be presented.

The idea in this chapter is to provide talking points for the administration in support of tween services. Ideally, previously completed community research will confirm that it makes sense for the library to have tween services. Sharing that information clearly and compellingly will be crucial when talking to the administration. It is also helpful to begin the communication process knowing the order in which to approach colleagues within the library's administration. Assuming the research inside and outside the library is done, it is time to present.

The first talking point can be about having an intermediary step between the children's department and the young adult department. This intermediary step will take the form of collection, programming, and potentially other services directed specifically at tweens. This is where some of the community research is going to come in. If other community groups are organized to include certain age groups, then that will inform how the library groups its tweens. Also, when talking to the administration, being able to say "Patrons have told me ..." or "I have overheard customers chatting about ..." when it has to do with organizing collections or services can provide extra support for one's ideas. Make sure there is anecdotal evidence from the community as well as research that supports the plan being proposed. Anecdotal evidence from parents in the community and their ideas about what they want also make a compelling case. Make sure these stakeholders are telling someone their ideas, concerns, and wishes.

Tween materials tend to address two types of parental concerns. In a really exaggerated sense, they are "My child is more advanced in reading, but I don't want him/her reading Danielle Steel," and "I'm not ready for my child to read books with sex, drugs, and rock and roll." The wonderful thing is that this means there are parents who really care about their children and what they are reading. Libraries want parents involved in their children's lives. If there are enough community comments of this kind, there can be a real case for creating a tween section of materials, which means taking materials from the children's and young adult departments and creating a tween department.

Intermediary programming serves a similar function. Tweens can be very mature one moment and very childish the next. While this idea was discussed in earlier chapters, it bears repeating here. It is difficult for parents of tweens to know what programs are best for their children. Providing programs that appeal to the changing maturity levels of tweens can allow both children's and young adult programs to be stable in their focus and audience, leaving tween programming to be more variable.

The second talking point is going to be primarily programming based. Tween programs, because they account for the changing maturity of this age group, are more likely to keep tweens returning to the library. Children's programs may be perceived as "too childish," and young adult programs as "too old." Traditionally the age ranges assigned to tweens are advertised when there is another huge crop of potential activities that become available to these individuals. It is in the library's best interests to be as interesting and relevant as possible within the range of things going on. In talking with the administration, highlight the types of services that the library can provide to tweens in the building that are not being covered within the other activities of the community.

Keep in mind, and potentially include in the persuasive points, that tween programs will give children "aging out" of successful children's programs something new to do until they are ready for the great young adult programs that the library provides; in this way, tweens and their families will remain attached to the library. The library wants children to be excited to attend tween activities and, eventually, young adult activities. Ideally, parents should also feel comfortable bringing their tweens to the library for programs.

No matter what, keep the focus of the message on how tween services will better serve the community. This is always the goal. Research has been done, and patrons in the community have shared ideas. Talking to tweens themselves provides additional depth to the message. What will the library gain by having tween services?

This is now the second part of the persuasive presentation. Ideally the administration will hear that the library will get a whole lot without having to spend much money. What will the library gain? Visibility within the community? More people in the library? Better circulation of materials? Be sure to know what the administration wants and demonstrate how tween services will work toward those specific goals.

If the library wants more visibility in the community, a new section of materials can do that. If marketed and publicized well, this can be a great way for the library to respond to the needs of the community. If there can be input and suggestions from tweens and their parents about what materials will go in the new tween section and what programming can be conducted, then publicizing the fact that community guidance was received can also go over really well. Most libraries want to be visible in their communities and be perceived as part of the community.

If the administration wants more people in the library, a robust programming schedule of activities that appeal to tweens should be able to achieve that goal. Get help from tweens themselves or their parents to provide suggestions of things to do that would be successful in bringing more people to the library. Just be careful to not duplicate programming that is going on elsewhere in the community. It is not good practice to compete with another organization for the same bodies in the building.

There is not a library around that does not want increased circulation of materials. This can come from good marketing and publicity, but it will also come from word of mouth. Parents talk at the soccer field, and children talk in school. Wherever the tweens and their parents in the community gather, they will talk about where they got the book that was required for school or how their library has extra copies of a particular book since it is the new, hot tween title. Make sure that the community knows that the librarians have worked hard for their tweens and made their needs a priority in the tween section.

Remember, when talking to the administration, be positive. Know the information. Do not be discouraged if the answer is "no" the first time around. Make sure to do research and be prepared for all outcomes.

The Takeaway

- Focus on how tween services will make for a seamless continuum of library services.
- Emphasize what benefits the library will gain from specific tween services.
- Be prepared, especially if the initial response is not too supportive.

6

Gaining Support
from Your Staff

For the majority of this book, the focus is on the tween librarian, talking about different aspects of tween services from his or her perspective. However, in this chapter, tween services is approached from the perspective of an administrator interested in creating a new position, collection, and services to meet tweens' specific needs. What is it about tween services that would be a good fit for your library?

As an administrator, it may seem that the library is in need of tween services. What gave rise to this idea? Is tween services a way to provide programs for young patrons slipping through the cracks between children's activities and those for young adults? Do tween materials need to be kept in a separate collection for the benefit of patrons who want to be neither in the babyish children's area nor in the mature young adult area? Is providing tween services in general a good idea based on how things are organized in the community? Any or all of these can be reasons to pursue tween services. When talking to the staff members and telling them why the library needs tween services, what is in it for them? If the staff now needs to provide these services, the reason had better not be "Do this or be fired!" There should be a more compelling explanation.

Look at the existing staff. Are there staff members who have gifts and talents that could be brought to bear on tween programming? That is the ideal situation. Make sure when presenting this idea to the intended programmer or group of programmers that there is an emphasis on the gifts that would be best utilized in providing tween services. Make sure the staff knows that the administration, whether that is one person or many, think they are important and have something of value to offer other people. Perhaps, as the administrator, there is the possibility of shifting responsibilities among staff members. Are there some who are more interested in providing programming than reference or collection development? A shifting of assignments that ends up benefiting the administration and some other staff as well would be perfect. Enter the conversation with a willingness to talk and collaborate with staff. They may have other ideas, especially if it is something that sounds appealing.

Perhaps there is a specific person in mind to provide tween services. As an administrator, is there someone who needs a new challenge? Tween services may be just the thing. Oftentimes a newer staff member will be thrilled to have the opportunity to create something from practically nothing. Tween services can be a challenge, since tweens are not nearly as easy to define as children or teenagers. However, if there seems to be someone who has the makings of a good tween librarian, then go ahead and try it. There is more information in a later chapter about the ideal tween librarian, but give him or her the opportunity to create something new and make it their own.

The real challenge for an administrator is when there does not appear to be anyone currently on staff who is jumping at the chance to provide tween services. Is there a way to show the existing staff that the continuum of youth services is not continuous? Someone on staff now has the opportunity to provide a missing piece in the continuum. Everyone's contribution to the continuum is important, and finding a way to make sure everyone has an individual and equally special part of that task is the job of the administrator. Make sure that the staff understands where they fit in the bigger picture, whether these are staff members who are now serving a smaller age range of youths as a result of creating specific tween services or the person who is working with the tweens. Sometimes it helps to literally draw a number line (or, in this case, an age line) and put everyone's name there to show where they are and where their contributions are. Everyone has a different role to play.

If, in the end, the decision is made to hire someone new to provide tween services, examine the candidates carefully. Think about how to successfully integrate this person into the rest of the staff. Existing staff may be resistant to a new person coming in to do something different. Be sensitive to everyone's feelings and needs to be respected and acknowledged as the professionals they are.

Assuming there is someone interested in providing tween services, they need to be provided with the resources to do that. The primary resource is going to be money. It will more than likely be necessary to talk with the existing staff about why they do not have as much money as they used to because some of it has been diverted to tween services. Even if it turns out that the person who will be providing tween services is also responsible for money intended for children's or young adult services, it is best for tween services to have separate money for materials and programming. This will ensure that each area of the continuum has dedicated funds to use to make it successful.

Having gotten a tween services person and set aside resources for that person to use, where will tween services be located? Is there a separate collection of materials somewhere? Exactly where is that place, especially in relation to children's and teen materials? These are questions an administrator must answer and explain to the staff. Again, talking to people about how the physical space they oversee has gotten smaller because part has now become a space for tweens can be difficult. Remember that the emphasis should always be on serving patrons better and having a continuum of youth services. Be prepared to roll up one's sleeves (probably literally) and help the staff move shelves, books, or whatever is necessary to create the new tween area. As an administrator, commitment to this new service will be demonstrated to the staff more by this action than any other.

Finally, it will be necessary to talk with the staff about how to publicize tween services and gain the support of the community for this new idea. As has been said earlier, talk about the continuum of services and how much there is to gain through providing for this group of patrons. Take the time to listen to the staff, especially when they think no one is listening. While no one is advocating sneaking up on the staff or hiding somewhere and eavesdropping, there is hope that a culture can be developed with the staff in which they feel comfortable asking questions and talking about things in a way that is respectful of differing opinions. The staff could strive to make the tween services venture unsuccessful if they are not convinced that it is in their best interests to support this new idea. Make the investment of time. The reward will be successful tween services in your library provided by your already awesome and talented staff.

The Takeaway

- Show the library staff why tween services are important by explaining what they could gain from it.
- Finding the best person to be the tween librarian can take quite a bit of time and effort.
- Be prepared to answer questions from your staff about tween services and literally plan to help launch tween services with your staff when it's time.

7

Collegial Support
for Tween Services

As mentioned before, it may be necessary to get the support of one's colleagues before approaching the administration. However, the tactics are fairly similar in both cases. Approaching colleagues also starts with research and knowing the community, so that they can be convinced of the benefits of tween services. The other thing to consider with colleagues is the benefit of having their support through the inevitable bumps and setbacks that come with trying something new. Depending on the interpersonal dynamics of the department or library, it may be an important long-term investment to take a little time at the beginning of the process to make sure colleagues support the addition of tween services.

A good place to start is thinking about how tween services can lighten the load or simplify colleagues' work lives and responsibilities. Colleagues who do children's programming are probably going to be the first people to get on your side. Sometimes tweens still want to go to storytime, particularly younger tweens, as they are still at that point where the stories and activities are fun. Or they may be reaching a point in their lives when they still want to do things that might be perceived as younger because there is some other part of growing up they do not want to deal with. Some libraries have family storytimes or other "all ages" programming that really does not ultimately end up appealing to the tweens. However, having the opportunity to do a special tween storytime where the books and the activities are more age appropriate can really help colleagues who might be conducting similar programs with very wide age spreads.

It is not that what colleagues are doing for children (and tweens) is bad. Choose your words carefully when speaking with colleagues, because it is so easy to have a message misinterpreted. However, asking colleagues who conduct programs with wide age spreads to describe their favorite age groups to work with or their favorite library programs may provide an opening to the conversation about beginning dedicated tween services. Talking with colleagues about what they enjoy doing will hopefully provide the opportunity to help them by saying there could be someone to do special programs for this other age group, assuming that they ultimately end up saying that they do not prefer tweens. However, if it turns out that they love working with tweens, now there is one more cheerleader and advocate for tween services. More importantly, there is now a program collaborator within the library. Tween services could now be provided by two people instead of just one. Be open to what colleagues are saying. It is possible to learn more than simply their opinions on tweens.

Remember that one of the primary reasons for tween programming is to bridge the gap between children's and young adult programming. Discuss with young adult librarian colleagues which participants seem too young for their programs, or what they would like to do in programs that they cannot because they have too many younger kids. This will be very similar to the conversation with the children's programming people. We do not mean to imply that tweens are the castoffs of either the children's or the young adult departments. Tweens, as mentioned many times before, are their own very diverse and hard-to-describe creatures. Giving them their own programs is just good library service.

There is a good chance that colleagues who work with young adults will be much more willing to let someone else provide tween programming than children's librarian colleagues. There is no good reason why this would be the case, but based on anecdotal evidence from many other librarians at different libraries, this seems to be common. Remember that the message to colleagues is about providing quality programming to a cross section of youths who may view themselves as not fitting exactly into either children's or young adult departments in a library. Stick to the message!

Also keep in mind while talking to colleagues on either end of the programming age spectrum that, as the person providing tween library services, the opportunity to collaborate with these people on programming is great. Keep using the concept of a continuum of library service, in which everyone helps each other move patrons from baby time to preschool storytime to elementary programs to tween programs to young adult programs. However, if the concept of a continuum does not work, there is another way to look at this situation. For people doing children's programming, helping with tween programs is an opportunity to spend "one last time" with their favorite maturing elementary school children now becoming tweens. It is also an opportunity to introduce the tween librarian to their beloved library children. The same is true when the young adult programming people get help from the tween programmer, only this time it is the tween librarian providing the introduction to the young adult program leaders as they meet the new teenagers.

Of course, this does not mean that programming that covers a broad age range of attendees is no more. There are many reasons to continue to have activities with wide age spans. Tween programming is just a way to diversify offerings and try to reach more people. Be sensitive to your colleagues. Tween services is an attempt to help them and the patrons. It is always about better helping patrons.

As far as materials go, purchasing specifically tween materials can also be a challenge. More than likely the library is not going to magically find money without taking it from somewhere else. There may be colleagues who will not be happy at the prospect of giving some of their money to be used specifically for tween materials.

If money is not an issue, it may just be that they do not want to give the collection development control to someone else. Remind them that tween services is making their jobs easier by allowing them to concentrate their efforts and expertise in a narrower band of the collection.

A specific tween collection can become appealing to colleagues who will be able to direct anxious or concerned parents and tweens past the babyish children's materials and not into the very mature young adult area. This cannot be stressed enough— "tween" is the middle ground in the continuum of youth services. There will now be a place to send people who need the "middle ground" material. If the library is within a community that is prone to book challenges because someone perceives a book as inappropriate for the section it is in, a tween materials section may be a perfect way to lessen these events.

Lest anyone believe that the only colleagues who must be convinced that tween services are important are fellow youth services colleagues, it is necessary to look at some additional people in the library. The next group to talk to and get support from are the people who work with adults. On the surface, this may seem odd, since working with adults is quite different from the challenges of working with youths, but these colleagues will be in contact with the parents of tweens. If they can be convinced of the benefits that specific tween services will bring to the library, then these people can advocate to parents and other adult patrons who may not understand. Think more critically about how tween services may personally impact the day-to-day work of adult services librarians. One argument might be "Special tween programs may attract the tweens who are here already to attend the program instead of sitting here in the adult area." Again, anecdotal evidence suggests that oftentimes adult services people would just as soon not see any child, young or old, in their area of the library. Creating a space that attracts tweens and keeps them from roaming to other parts of the library can establish some more supporters for tween services.

Whether materials are processed by a book vendor or whether it happens at the library, talk with the people on staff who process books. Ask them about creating a tween-specific collection. How would they suggest labeling it? How can it be noted in the public access catalogs so patrons of all ages know where to find the materials? Just as the old adage says about going to management with a solution to a problem, not just a problem, have some suggestions ready for surmounting potential obstacles. Ultimately, the idea you propose may not be the solution chosen, but approaching the book-processing team with potential remedies is helpful. Also, keep in mind that the people who process books might not often be consulted about changes affecting them but instead just have to react to the changes. Some of them may be parents of tweens or part of the community, and their support of tween services could help quite a bit. Make them part of the cheerleading squad for tween services.

It may not be immediately obvious that the people who work at the circulation desk are important ones to win over to the cause of tween services. However, they are. Sometimes these individuals have more contact with patrons than anyone else in the library. It is beneficial to have the circulation staff talk up the amazing new service that the library is offering to everyone who comes in the door. What about having specific tween services in the library will make their work lives easier? Will it give marauding tweens something to do instead of congregating in front of the circulation desk? Will the new tween materials area give the circulation folks a specific place to which to direct patrons who need materials for their 9-to-14-year-old? Are there people who work in the circulation department who have tweens? Will this help them in their personal lives? Just as with the staff members who process books, the circulation people may not be used to someone from youth services coming over and talking specifically to them. Everyone who works in the library is important, and making sure that the circulation folks understand what is happening and are on board can be essential for your new venture.

Look at the library's organizational chart. Who has been missed? What about talking to the maintenance people or security folks? Will having separate tween services impact their jobs? Are you expecting that the maintenance people will help move shelving and furniture to create the new space? If so, then explain to them what will happen and why their help is invaluable. Is there separate security in the library? With the change to specific tween services, will the security person need to change his or her rounds through the building? Make sure security knows what the tween space will look like. Don't let it be a surprise.

Are there more people to approach? What about talking to the people who handle finances, human resources, or marketing, or those who put away books and materials for the library? Does the finance person know that there will be a separate budget for tween services? Do not wait to have someone from administration talk to them. Be proactive. Maybe they will have some helpful information that has not been mentioned yet. Additionally, if new library services have been created, does that mean that a new job description is necessary? That will probably be something that the human resources person is involved in. Make sure to talk to him or her, even if it is just to provide an alert that an administrator will be talking to them about it sometime soon. Another powerful ally will be the person who works in marketing. After all, the new tween services will need to be publicized. Depending on the size of the library, individual staff may be expected to do this on their own, or the library may have a marketing and/or public relations person (or perhaps an entire team of people). If someone else is publicizing tween services, then they will need to understand as much as possible about what will be happening. The better they understand it, the better they can publicize it. They need to be the captain of the tween services cheerleading squad. And finally, do not forget the people who put away materials. If materials will be moving around to create a tween collection, let them know what to expect before it happens. Let them know where they will find materials and how the materials will be labeled. That shows respect for them, and in turn they will support the impending changes.

It may seem like talking to absolutely everyone in the library to get them to see how specific services for tweens will help the library as a whole is a lot of work. And it is. However, it is absolutely worth the time for several reasons. One, it is best to have everyone in the library be able to speak enthusiastically and supportively when asked by patrons about this new service when they are both inside the library and out in the community. Two, there will inevitably be down days. Everyone has them. The perfect program may self-destruct, or a parent may argue about how inappropriate they think a particular book is and why it does not belong in the tween section. At times like these, it may seem that the whole tween services thing is not a good idea. Let colleagues discuss why tween services are the right thing for the library to do. Finally, talking to everyone shows that their contributions are valued and their roles in the library are important. The tweens will also see how co-workers relate to each other. They see everything. It is impossible to treat tweens with consideration and then colleagues differently. Everyone in the library should respect one another.

The Takeaway

- Children's services colleagues will probably be the first group to approach about supporting the initiation of tween services.
- Make sure young adult services colleagues appreciate what they will gain by having tween services in the library.
- Talk to everyone in the library, from adult services to book processors and circulation clerks, because everyone can benefit from tween services.
- Making the investment to get all colleagues throughout the library to support tween services will benefit you in the long run.

8

Community Support
for Tween Services

As mentioned before, to begin tween services in the library, it may be beneficial to have the support of the community before approaching the administration. It always starts with knowing what will be gained by this new service. Who benefits from tween services, and why will it be good for this community to have tween services at their library? And what will be the best way to convince the community they need tween services?

Ideally the entire community will support having tween services at the library, but there are several key groups that absolutely must support the new offerings in order for tween services to succeed. These groups are the library board, the Friends group, library volunteers, the schools, and tweens' parents. The message to community stakeholders is really no different from the message to colleagues and library administration: tween services fills a particular niche in the continuum of youth services.

When talking to the library board, it is best to get advice ahead of time about how to present the idea. Depending on the board's structure, collectively they may just want the overview of what is happening, or they may wish to have some direct say in how things are carried out. Come to the board with a plan all laid out neatly, completely, and succinctly. Explaining about the developmental characteristics of tweens may help, but it may also be too much information. Talk about who tweens are in the community, and how the library will provide them with special services because they are too mature for the children's department and not mature enough for the young adult area. It may be easier to refer to tweens by grade level or, depending on the school systems, as middle school, junior high school, or upper elementary school students. Use words and phrases that mean something in the community. Make sure that the library board can easily see why this is a great idea for their library.

The Library Friends are people devoted to the library. They do all kinds of things that support the library's mission. Frequently Library Friends, or sometimes a library foundation, will provide monetary support for certain aspects of youth services, usually programming. Make sure that at least the Friends board knows what is happening at the library. The Friends are out in the community as part of other organizations, and it is helpful for them to be able to tell people about how their library is providing services for tweens so that youths of all ages will receive quality services appropriate for their developmental levels. Make sure the Friends support tween services, especially if the intention is to ask them for money for some aspect of starting up the new tween area. They may be providing a one-time monetary donation for new furniture or additional computers or something that will make the new tween space inviting and supportive of the materials and programming that will occur for this age group. Who knows—Friends volunteers may help move books from their existing locations to the new tween materials area.

Some libraries have volunteers, and some libraries do not. These adults may or may not be part of the Library Friends group. However, they are also people who believe in the library so much that they give of their time to help it be successful. Make sure that all volunteers (assuming the library has them) know what is going on in the library. Depending on how volunteers are organized, there may be a gathering to attend where a presentation about tween services can be made. This presentation should be simple, concise, and upbeat. Be ready to answer questions, because the volunteers will have them. Have multiple ways to explain the age level for tweens and why they do not fit perfectly as children or young adults. Be prepared to give examples of the kinds of materials that will be in the tween area and the types of programs that will be specifically intended for tweens. Provide a handout of key talking points for the volunteers. Whether they realize it or not, and they probably do, many of their friends and other people in the community look to them for information about the library, instead of asking the library staff. Make sure that the volunteers have the best and most correct information.

There are lots of people to talk to within the organization of the local schools around the library. Who are the best people to approach? Unfortunately, that is going to change district by district. In one district you might need to explain what library service for tweens is to the assistant superintendent or superintendent; then this person or persons will push the information down through the rest of the district. More than likely, talking to the principals and teachers who work with tweens will be the first step. They will benefit from the library offering tween services, but they may have additional information about tweens in the community that will be helpful. Talking about tween services and how it is part of the continuum of service to youths will be a message that schools can understand because they educate children from kindergarten through twelfth grade. Listen to what they have to say and make sure they understand that the library wants to support what they are doing with tweens in school. If there has not been a good relationship with the school before beginning dedicated tween services, this might be the opening necessary to develop a deep, long-lasting relationship that will benefit both groups.

The final and most important group within the community that needs to give the library support are the parents of the tweens themselves. As was noted in earlier chapters, tweens still depend on their parents for transportation, and while they want to be independent of their parents, these adults still wield a lot of power over what their children are doing. Start with the parents of current children's program attendees. Some of these children may actually be tweens who still want and need to come to library programs, but they may have aged out of other library offerings and are developmentally too young for teen programs. Some parents do not want their children to grow up too fast, so having something that isn't too babyish but doesn't put their "baby" with a bunch of high school students may be an attractive alternative to not doing programs at the library at all. Sometimes a separate collection of tween materials will attract the parents of tweens to the idea of separate services. They may be reluctant to go with their tween to look for books where the high schoolers are, and, as parents, they may need to do a lot more evaluating of the materials that come from that area if they believe that much of it is not appropriate for their child. They may also be hearing from their tweens that they don't want to be with the "little kids" in the children's area, since they are too mature for the books that are there. In some instances, talking briefly to parents about the developmental aspects of tweens that separate them from both children and teens may be helpful. However, there is a fine line to walk with that conversation, as it is detrimental to appear to be talking down to parents and act as though you know more about their child than they do. The other thing to do when talking about how tweens are more mature than children but not as mature as teens is lay the groundwork with the parents who will want to send their tween's third-grade sibling into the tween program as well. Remember, the message is about how tweens have special needs of their own. This point will be used over and over again with parents of tweens.

There are lots of other groups in the community whose support will be helpful for tween services; these are just a few. It is also good to remember the concept of the "the thirty-second elevator speech" (that is, a speech that is compressed into the time frame of a typical elevator ride). Make sure this pitch is ready for whenever anyone is out in the community. News travels fast and in ways that cannot be predicted. Always be prepared to talk to whoever asks about tween services, so that everyone will know how tween services is a good thing for the library and the community.

The Takeaway

- There are many community stakeholders who will benefit from tween services, but they need to understand what that means.
- Making sure the Library Friends and volunteers know about and support tween services is important because they will be ambassadors of the message to the rest of the community.
- Do not forget that parents of tweens are important stakeholders and need to see all the wonderful things that will come from separating tweens from children's services and young adult services.

SECTION III

Creating and Caring for the Tween Librarian

This section details who a tween librarian is and how that person will continue to grow in the job. These are two very important ideas because once a tween librarian has been procured, it is important for that person to continue to develop in the position.

The first chapter describes the ideal tween librarian. The intent is to outline character traits and allow the reader to evaluate whether this applies to himself or herself personally or describes the kind of person who would fit well into a current library's staff. This may be the chapter that helps the reader decide, "No. This whole tween librarian thing is definitely not for me." Ideally the reader will complete the chapter and think, "Oh, my goodness. They wrote this chapter about me. How do they know so much about me?" However, if the reader decides this chapter describes a colleague, the hope is that this person will be encouraged to consider providing library services to tweens.

The second chapter is about continuing education. This subject comes relatively early in the book because being a tween librarian can sometimes get lonely. It definitely takes a bit of art and a bit of luck to find sources of inspiration and growth as a tween librarian. It can feel overwhelming and worrisome as plans for tween services progress. The idea is to plan for support early in the process and avoid feeling isolated.

9

Who Is the Ideal
Tween Services Librarian?

Is there a universal definition of what makes the best tween librarian? Probably not. The lack of a definite consensus on precisely what ages represent tweens makes describing what or who a tween librarian is even more difficult. However, as with many things stated earlier in this book, the description of an ideal tween librarian is going to be very community specific. What works in one locality may not work in another. Therefore, this section covers elements that may be found in an ideal tween librarian, but not everything will apply in every community.

A good tween librarian is part children's librarian and part young adult librarian. This person can effortlessly adapt to the changing moods of the library's tweens. This person is sort of like a boy band—slightly edgy but something a mom can listen to in the car. However, what does that actually mean? Looking at elements of a job advertisement will allow an examination of the different characteristics of a tween librarian.

Education

As with many other things connected with tweens, there is no consensus regarding what kind of educational background an ideal tween librarian will have. While having a bachelor's degree (or even a master's degree) in education (either elementary or secondary education) is ideal, it's not required. However, if there isn't formal training in how to work with children, a potential candidate must have something on his or her resume that demonstrates experience in this area. It could be babysitting, serving as a camp counselor or teacher's aide, teaching religious classes, working at a summer camp, or something like that. Even better would be several different child-related experiences in which the ages of the children vary. This is going to be where candidates who have a degree in education will potentially edge out the people who do not. Generally most degree programs have students in several different placements with a wide range of children (of all ages). Thus, by the time they get their degree they have a general idea of how different aged children behave. However, when looking at resumes of potential candidates, don't automatically throw out everyone whose bachelor's degree is anything but education.

Section III. Creating and Caring for the Tween Librarian

Does the perfect tween librarian have an MLIS? That is up to individual libraries. There are a few (but fortunately growing in number) classes or workshops in master's degree programs that focus on working with tweens. Of course, one weekend workshop on providing library services to tweens does not a tween librarian make. However, what a master's degree can provide for a potential tween librarian is broader training in literature for different ages. That will serve the candidate well, but following a prescribed path to become either a children's librarian or a young adult librarian will leave some gaps in knowledge that will need to be compensated for when looking for a potential tween librarian.

Since tweens are not an easily defined age group, the ideal tween librarian will need to have a decent background in things that are child-related and teen-related. What does this mean exactly? Strictly from a literature perspective, a good tween librarian will be conversant in books that can be read by people who range from a second-grade through tenth-grade reading level. The reason for the huge reading span is that tweens are at the point where reading can change (especially for boys) to being more work and less fun. It is often at this stage that reluctant readers are developed, as well as voracious readers. This can also be the time when children are formally labeled as below grade level or above grade level in terms of reading ability. It is not unusual to see a fourth grader, a nine- to ten-year-old, reading at a second-grade reading level. And on the other end of the spectrum you can have a seventh grader, a twelve- or thirteen-year-old, reading at a tenth-grade reading level or higher. Fortunately (or unfortunately), an ideal tween librarian is going to have a broad knowledge of youth literature, potentially more than a children's librarian or young adult librarian might need to have, although the idea of needing to know a very broad range of literature, from the *Magic Tree House* series through the newest John Greene tearjerker, is a bit daunting.

Experience

Sometimes there are big differences between education and real-world experience. Occasionally a person may actually have relevant experience but, for whatever reason, does not include it on a resume. However, given the range of ages and developmental stages that mark the tween group, becoming a tween librarian is probably not a good "first library job." An ideal candidate will have worked in libraries in other capacities first, in either paraprofessional or professional positions. Given the amount of collaboration and teamwork that comes with being a tween librarian, an ideal candidate needs to have a good idea of how libraries operate in general before becoming a tween librarian.

Collaboration is huge for a tween librarian. As far as it relates to hiring, an ideal candidate will have demonstrable experience working in groups or teams. This topic will probably come up during the interview. A potential tween librarian is going to need to work closely with both the library staff who do programming and collections for children and those who do the same things for teens. If possible, these people should be involved somehow in the interview process for the new tween librarian.

Job Requirements

There are a few other questions that will help define the ideal tween librarian. For example, is this a full-time or part-time position? And what exactly is the tween librarian doing? Is it just programming, or is it collections too? Is the tween librarian responsible for outreach activities? What role will the tween librarian play within the larger library organization? In some ways, the later questions will determine whether the tween librarian is a full-time or part-time position; in a best-case scenario the tween librarian will be a full-time employee. There are a couple reasons for this.

Ideally the tween librarian will be immersed in everything tween at the library, including doing collection development and weeding the tween collection (which in a perfect world would contain tween books, movies, magazines, and music). Managing the collection and making sure it is current and popular takes a lot more time than it seems like it should sometimes. However, it is most certainly time well spent. In addition, there are programming aspects of being a tween librarian. That means this person, scheduling wise, is going to need to be available afternoons, evenings, and weekends. Basically, whenever the tweens are out of school, that could be a time for a program. However, outreach to tweens is definitely going to include a school visit component, which usually means mornings. There are a lot of things that a tween librarian could be involved in, and that is before adding in the need to collaborate with others and probably work at a reference desk. It is also going to include time for advocacy among colleagues and in the greater community to understand and support tween activities, because sometimes tweens are a bit too prickly to easily love.

Personality or Knowledge Required

Ideally the personality of a tween librarian is something you can discern in a new hire and determine whether there are certain building blocks to start out with. There are things that can be taught to a person with time, but there are other things a good tween librarian is going to need to have before the job starts. An awareness of pop culture is a must. Obviously a person can prepare before an interview by reading social media sites or entertainment news websites. However, the idea is that an ideal tween librarian should be familiar with pop culture. Of course, he or she doesn't have to know everything, since there is nothing tweens (and actually most children) love more than to know something that adults do not. And the opportunity to have a tween teach the librarian something is always beneficial for everyone.

Section III. Creating and Caring for the Tween Librarian

A good tween librarian is going to be self-aware and have a certain amount of confidence or bravado. Being self-aware in this case means knowing what you know, knowing what you don't know, and knowing whom you can go to for back-up or help. Unfortunately, self-awareness comes with age and experience—another reason why tween librarian might not be the best "first job." The confidence (or bravado) is necessary because tweens are like dogs: they can smell fear and unease. If the tween librarian is not sure what is going on or what to do (or who to go to for assistance), the tweens will sense it and take advantage of this weakness. We cannot stress enough that being able to ask for help and knowing that help will be provided is a huge part of having a successful tween librarian.

Another element of awareness that a tween librarian must have is knowledge of the community. This is not something that the person must have before the interview, but eventually it will be part of his or her job. A tween librarian must know, first and foremost, whom the community considers a tween. However, knowing where they hang out, what is available in the community to do for fun, and what community sports rivalries exist is also extremely helpful. This is where colleagues can help support the tween librarian and point him or her in the correct direction early on.

The implication so far is that a new tween librarian will come from outside the existing library staff, and maybe even outside the community, but that may not always be the case. There may be someone already on staff who would fit the criteria quite well. Do not be surprised if it's a current children's or young adult librarian looking for a change in age group. There are a lot of advantages to hiring "in house." It's possible that this person has been training and growing into a wonderful tween librarian without really knowing it. In addition, a current staff person already should know a fair amount about the community, and that probably includes knowing the children.

Miscellaneous Ideas to Consider

Before making a final decision, consider training and support after hiring. The new tween librarian, especially if he or she is the first person in a newly created position, is going to need support from colleagues and the administration as he or she develops his or her individual tween librarian style. That means there will be mishaps and mistakes. Much more can be learned from mistakes than successes, but it can be a disheartening and upsetting process. There needs to be a safety net for the new person and position.

The discussion about hiring a tween librarian would not be complete without some mention of technological capabilities. A tween librarian does not have to be a technological wizard, knowing every single new advance the day it comes out. However, being familiar with and moderately capable in using the library's different technologies, as well as being aware of new technologies (especially regarding how they relate to the library), is crucial. Additionally, a tween librarian might want to become acquainted with the library's IT staff because this person or group may be able to help and support the tween librarian down the road.

The Takeaway

Whether you hire from within the current library staff or advertise and choose someone from the outside, knowing what the tween librarian will be doing and, ideally, what personality traits you want are important before beginning the hiring process. Sometimes a person's resume may be misleading; interviews help quite a bit. A good tween librarian is a combination of a superhero and "practically perfect in every way" like Mary Poppins.

A good tween librarian:

- will be interested in providing library services to all youths, from birth through high school graduate;
- will have a lot of experiences working with children prior to entering the library field;
- will probably have been either a children's or a young adult librarian but may not have acquired an MLIS degree;
- will concentrate on collections, programming, and outreach for tweens, which may or may not be a full-time job (depending on the library);
- will be able to collaborate with others both in the library and in the community;
- will carry him- or herself with poise and confidence, not unlike a stage actor; and
- will possibly be chosen from the annotated job description provided below but more than likely will be hired based on a description that best fits the community.

Partial (and Annotated) Tween Librarian Job Description

Most library job descriptions start with something about the culture of the library or the department the prospective hire will be working in. Some job descriptions overall are very short, and others are quite long.

PRIMARY DUTIES:

- This is whatever is going to be most important to the library. Will this person be first and foremost a collection development librarian, or is the primary job programming? Perhaps the priority is outreach. Make sure that whatever your library views as most important is listed first.

Section III. Creating and Caring for the Tween Librarian

- Will this person work at the reference desk at all? Is it the children's reference desk? Adult reference desk? Is all reference for all ages handled at the same location?
- This person is going to need to collaborate with other staff, but how much and with whom is up to the particular library. Tell perspective candidates up front what they should expect in terms of collaboration. A person who works better as a lone wolf will recognize early on that this is not a good fit if the description explicitly states that collaboration is necessary.
- There are many duties that can be described, but if there are things that are expected of all librarians or all library staff, it is best to spell that out here. It could be that every person is an ambassador of the library and, as such, certain activities and behaviors are non-negotiable.
- It is good to spell out basic technology responsibilities here. Otherwise, they will get lost in other parts of the job description.
- Will this person be responsible for doing his or her own marketing of tween activities and collections, or is there someone else on staff who does that? In the case of the latter, will the tween librarian collaborate with this person?
- Including something here about staying current in the field, whether that is professional literature or continuing education, is particularly important for tween librarians.

QUALIFICATIONS (sometimes called experience or knowledge):
1. It is up to individual libraries to decide whether they want an MLIS degree holder.
2. Individual libraries will also need to determine whether they want to specify a certain bachelor's degree or types of degrees required.
3. A tween librarian should have demonstrable experience working with tweens. It is helpful to spell out here (if it has not been done elsewhere) the ages of the tweens in the community. How much experience is necessary is an individual library's decision.
4. It may be advantageous to have candidates possess a working knowledge of tween literature before they are hired, but teaching about literature is fairly easy, so it may not be a required element at the time of hire.
5. There are probably some standard qualifications that are common to all librarians or employees of a particular library, and that would go here as well.

There are probably other items that need to go in the job description. Whoever handles HR-related tasks at the library should be able to help fill in the gaps in the newly developed job description.

10

Continuing Education

It has been mentioned several times already, but one of the challenges of being a tween librarian is finding other people who are tween librarians. And, again, tweens in each community are different. Being a tween librarian is really like being a detective—this person is always searching for what is the answer for the tweens in their community. It may be advisable (at least to start) to go into training situations knowing that maybe only a quarter of the "surefire" tween ideas that someone else has will work for one's own community.

Networking

Tween librarians absolutely must network with other librarians. This may be for their sanity more than anything else: they need to have people to talk to who will understand what they are going through. Unfortunately, it may not be clear who those peers are. Remember that, depending on the size of the library or library system, there may be ready-made understanding peers within the library. If the library is a standalone facility, a tween librarian may look to other libraries in the county or in the region to find the necessary collegial support. However, do not look for things that are labeled "for tween librarians" because there may not be much. Hopefully there will start to be more things that are specifically intended for those who work with tweens, but in the meantime tween librarians will have to investigate more.

At least initially, going to networking events or workshops for young adult and/or children's librarians is wise. This is how tween librarians will start to get a feel for what topics are discussed within both of these groups and where they, as tween librarians, might fit in. Keep in mind that, at least for the foreseeable future, the tween librarians may have to attend both types of events because usable information can be collected from such gatherings. Unfortunately, no one has as much time as they would like to devote to continuing education. Trying to attend programs and events for both children's and young adult librarians means a tween librarian could potentially be attending vastly more educational offerings than other colleagues who are responsible for either children's or young adult programs. It is best to be judicious about what is chosen. Try to select events that have the potential to provide the greatest benefit possible.

If it has not been mentioned in some other context outside of this book, here is a valuable piece of information: in many cases, more learning occurs during the lunch, breakfast, networking, or chit-chatting portions of the event than during the actual program itself. It is in sitting with different people at lunch exchanging "war stories" that tween librarians find individuals who understand them and have work circumstances similar to their own. As they start to find these people at events, that may indicate whether children's programs or young adult programs have more benefit for them.

Tweens are so community specific that it is far more difficult to get good advice from colleagues about this age group than it is for colleagues who work with high schoolers or preschoolers, which are more narrowly and consistently defined age groups. However, in order to get helpful suggestions from colleagues, be honest about what works in the community and what does not. That can sometimes be a challenge, because being honest about the community while helping to plan programming and determine the types of materials to include can seem a bit disrespectful to the community's image in a broader area. Remember that the tween librarian's job is to do the best work for the community and the people within it. Meet them where they are and support them in what they are doing and what they need. Just keep in mind that in order to do this as gently as possible, tween librarians must talk about their community with the same compassion and respect that they show when talking to the tweens themselves.

Available Resources

Some potential resources are local, regional, statewide, national, or even virtual. And, of course, there may be resources outside of the public library realm that may be useful. Finally, do not forget that the community's tweens will be more than happy to help instruct their librarian. They are always willing to share their knowledge with someone who is willing to listen.

Local Continuing Education

Perhaps "continuing education" is not quite the right term for the knowledge gained from local librarians, whether part of the library system, surrounding systems, or stand-alone libraries. Depending on how libraries are organized in the area, tween librarians may be able to attend meetings of local children's or young adult librarians. Reach out to colleagues who may know other library professionals. And if there is not a gathering of local children's or young adult librarians, create one. There is nothing that says a tween librarian cannot create something new. Ideally, any new gathering should be for librarians serving youths of all ages; then it is only one event to attend instead of two! Local peers are going to understand better than anyone else what a particular tween librarian is going through because tweens are products of their environments. Even local tweens from different communities are probably fairly similar to each other.

Regional Continuing Education

Most states have some type of regional gatherings for youth services librarians. Do not forget the regional associations, which could be based on an interlibrary loan system or consortium membership. Conversely, a regional association could be a solely geographic organization that bands together to provide other services like continuing education. Again, remember to attend both programs for children and those for young adults. Also keep in mind that a regional association may provide access to webinars and things that can be done from a desk at work either in real time or asynchronously. Be open to the different possibilities that exist.

Statewide Continuing Education

On a state level there may be continuing education offered through the state library or through the statewide library association. Either of these entities may have resources or programs that will be of interest to a tween librarian. Most state libraries also have someone who specializes in youth programs. That person may have resources or contact names of people who could be helpful. The opportunity to interact with people from vastly different geographic areas provides many different ideas to consider because of their varied communities. Most statewide library associations have at least annual conferences that provide a wealth of workshops to attend in a short amount of time. These could be held more regionally or at one location for the benefit of the whole state. Sometimes these conferences may require that the library or librarian be a member of the association or charge a significantly higher price to attend if they are not. Either way, these conferences can be expensive. However, information on workshops, speakers, and practically everything else that will be going on at the conference will be available ahead of time. Check the advance notifications to decide whether it appears that enough information can be gained from a given conference to justify the cost in money and time away from the library. At the state level, many places are starting to offer programs about tweens in libraries. It may be possible to just attend programs that are about tweens, making a state conference a good choice.

National Continuing Education

There is no denying that continuing education provided at the national level is some of the most monetarily expensive learning to have. There can be costs to belong to the national organization as well as to subgroups within it. However, with that said, there are three divisions of the American Library Association (ALA) that provide quality programs relating to tweens. The Association for Library Service to Children (ALSC) has been offering sessions at its biennial conference as well as during ALA Annual that are good for tween librarians (although they don't always include the word "tween" in the title). There are also ALSC webinars that provide information about serving tweens. The Young Adult Library Services Association (YALSA) provides information for librarians serving tweens in the same formats that ALSC does, by means of its biennial conference, sessions at ALA Annual, and webinars. However, YALSA may be more beneficial to you as a tween librarian if your tweens tend to be more mature either chronologically or emotionally. Finally, the Public Library Association (PLA) offers sessions about tweens at its conferences, most particularly its biennial conference, but not as much at ALA Annual.

The other thing to keep in mind is that the three divisions of ALA produce quite a bit of literature for their respective audiences. And of course ALA itself has a publication that relatively recently has included several articles about offering library services to tweens. Part of your continuing education will involve keeping up with the writings, both in print and online, about tweens.

Virtual Continuing Education

The label of "virtual continuing education" might be a bit of a misnomer; this is where we talk about making the most of listservs and social media. There are electronic discussion lists that you can become part of as a member of some of the ALA divisions. Another popular electronic discussion list is PUBYAC (PUBlic libraries for Young Adults & Children). Here, as on the ALA listservs, members can post questions and garner responses from library professionals across the country. PUBLIB is a third popular electronic discussion list, but since it is intended for all public librarians, it does not have as much information directly related to tweens. Sometimes state or regional organizations operate local electronic discussion lists, or librarians can join distribution lists in which potentially pertinent information is shared with the list members. There are also many Facebook groups that a tween librarian can become a part of; some are public groups, and others are closed. If they are closed, it does not mean that a person cannot request to be part of the group. Storytime Underground is a public Facebook group that is quite popular. Teen Think Tank and Teen Librarians are both closed groups that you can ask to join. What any virtual gathering of librarians provides is, again, a group of people who sympathize with and know what a librarian is going through. Reaching out to as many different types of people as possible helps combat the loneliness that comes with tween librarianship.

Continuing Education from Outside the Library Realm

Some of the largest resources that may be available to tween librarians for continuing education are groups and events targeting upper elementary and middle school teachers. While this may be a hard group to break into professionally because continuing education for teachers tends to be closed to outsiders, making friends with the middle school teachers and media center librarians may allow the tween librarian to be a guest at some of their workshops and gatherings. Once again, networking is crucial. Without contacts within the school community, a tween librarian may be unaware of or shut out from many events and opportunities. Even a simple lunch with staff from the middle school may be an invaluable learning experience and an excellent way to swap war stories or talk about interesting situations.

Learning from Tweens and Others in the Community

Do not discount the fact that tweens from the library are going to be able to tell their librarian what they are interested in. Sometimes that means doing a little research ahead of time to find out what the tweens are talking about. However, there is nothing wrong with letting them be the teachers. They may even be able to provide the names of people in the community who can be approached for more information about a particular topic, like art classes in the area or why certain programs are offered at the YMCA and not others. Tween librarians can learn a lot from people in the community who also work with tweens. Networking with them is important. Go out for coffee, and let the topic of tweens in the community guide the conversation to other important areas. Learning from the tweens is not continuing education in the strict sense of the term because it can mean learning about what cat videos on YouTube are the most popular or what music artist is the greatest ever, but it is valuable to learn from subject matter experts wherever they present themselves.

Final Thoughts

Currently there aren't a whole lot of dedicated tween librarian resources. However, any tween librarian can start a Facebook group or use some other sort of social media to get the ball rolling. Find a way to bring together other people who are also working to serve tweens. And if that does not work, apply to present at a conference, whether it is a regional, state, or national gathering. What is the worst that could happen? The program is not chosen—hardly a catastrophe. Also consider joining a committee on some level, and use that committee work as a way to search for others who are interested in tween services. Be creative. Do not be a lonely tween librarian.

The Takeaway

Just like forging the path to becoming a librarian for tweens and deciding what that means for the community, tween librarians must create their own path to continue learning and growing as professionals.

To find continuing education:

- network with other librarians serving the same age range (preferably a local group, if at all possible);
- initially visit education events for both children's librarians and young adult librarians;
- look to regional, statewide, and national education options to gain further information about tweens; and
- create continuing education opportunities if they not are already available.

SECTION IV

Setting the Stage for the Tween Collection

Getting a space for tween materials and getting tween materials to put in that space are sort of like the infamous chicken and egg question. What needs to happen first? Does a space come first, which will dictate how many materials can be obtained for the collection? Or do all the materials come first, followed by a search for a space that will hold them?

The first chapter in this section is about creating a tween space. In this discussion, shelving space is of primary importance. While there is some mention of furniture and other such things, the underlying assumption is that the tween space is being created "on the cheap," so (at least at the start) the focus is on finding somewhere to put the newly designated tween materials.

The second chapter has to do with deciding what materials from the existing youth collections are going to be part of the new tween collection. This includes books, periodicals, and audiovisual (AV) materials. However, particularly for AV materials, this description will err on the side of being fairly age conservative with how materials are placed into different age groups. Remember, each community has different ideas about what is appropriate for tweens.

11

Creating Your Tween Space

Where the tween collection is located, or even where in the building tween programming is conducted, can be a hot-button issue with the staff and community. Take time to get some feedback from different stakeholders, or at least be prepared with the reasoning for why things are placed where they are. Fortunately, many people can feel quite passionate about tweens, and these ideas may erupt here.

It cannot be said too often that knowing what the community thinks of the age group called tweens is critical. That has a lot to do with where the tweens will end up being housed within the library. This "no clear-cut location" challenge is indicative of the fact that tweens are on a sliding maturity scale. One day they are very mature, and another day they are not. Finding an appropriate location in the library can be a challenge for the tweens themselves, who may not know where they want to be from one day to the next, and it is even harder for their parents.

The first thing to realize is that the tween collection may be a smaller group of materials, at least at the outset. It is probably not going to be as large as the children's area or even the young adult area within the library. Figuring out approximately how many materials there might be in the new section is a good start before finding a place for them.

This is also a good time to do an inventory or thorough weeding of the youth collections to see what might be a good fit for the tweens (and also to determine what materials aren't being used). Since something physically will happen to each item to indicate that it is now part of the tween collection, it is a waste of effort and money to turn around and weed something for poor condition or non-use a few months after it was made into a tween book. In addition, weeding the entire collection will probably mean touching and looking at, albeit briefly, every book the library owns. This will help staff get a feel for what types of materials are available and what will become tween materials eventually. The tween materials should look appealing and have a fighting chance of being read in their new location, since they were being read in their previous location.

When there is an idea of approximately how many materials will be in the tween collection, determine whether there is enough room to put them somewhere in the library. In this case, this discussion is strictly a one of shelf space and how movable it might be. Ideally there will be empty shelves somewhere waiting to receive the "new" tween books, but more likely books will have to be shifted around as a new tween space is created. Can shelves be moved to the optimal location, or are the shelves bolted to the floor? Is it necessary to figure out where to make a tween section or it is fairly straightforward? Also, how high are the potential tween shelves? They can be taller than the shelves in the children's area, which primarily hold picture books. However, full-sized adult shelving is not advisable. Mid-range height, ideally similar to the height of the young adult shelving, would be perfect.

More than likely the tween section will be carved out of either the children's section or the young adult section, and each location can come with positive and negative aspects. Depending on where the new collection ends up, keep the following points in mind.

Being immediately adjacent to the young adult area comes with its own challenges. The positive aspect of this arrangement is that tweens will be near the "older kid" books and generally be inspired to read the more complex books because they want to be like the older teens. However, parents frequently are not thrilled that the young adult books, which can be more raw and cover a much wider range of topics, are so close to the tween books. While librarians can try very hard to police the language and topics of conversation that might come up within the stacks of young adult books among these patrons, parents of tweens may still have a problem with their children being exposed to such things. It more than likely will not bother the tweens because they hear it all the time, but parents may not want to know what their tween is hearing when he or she is out of the house.

Being immediately adjacent to the children's department has advantages and disadvantages as well. For parents, if there are multiple young children, it can mean that everyone is in approximately the same place, allowing parents to keep an eye on them more easily. It also means that, for young tweens especially, they are not mixing too much with the more worldly young adults who are probably in high school or possibly even trade school or college. However, for tweens who are desperate to be independent and separate from their families, being located so close to the "baby books" could leave them reluctant to make use of the collection.

While the majority of this chapter has been about separating tween fiction materials from their previous homes in the children's and young adult sections, it is necessary to give some thought to nonfiction materials. Does the library shelve all nonfiction, regardless of target audience age and reading level, in one place? Is there a separate nonfiction collection for children and young adults? If all nonfiction is shelved together, then there probably does not have to be anything changed about labeling or separating the tween materials from this area. However, if there is a children's nonfiction and an adult nonfiction collection, it may be best to leave things as they were.

Wherever the tween collection is located, good signage and publicity is key. It is also important to make sure all the library staff, reference librarians, circulation staff, pages, and even library volunteers understand where things have been moved and why. Ultimately, these will be the people who are asked about the move, not anyone who actually moved the materials. It is just the way things seem to turn out.

For some librarians, a tween space will be more than simply shelves to put tween materials on. Sometimes a little extra floor space comes as well, or even underutilized furniture from another part of the library. Do not look a gift horse in the mouth, to use the old cliché. Take whatever anyone is offering. If there is not any money to start out with, cast-offs are more than all right.

However, if there is money to spend on the organization and arrangement of the tween space, the most important thing is to talk with tweens about what they would like in their space. Do this before looking at a library furniture website or flipping through a catalog. The tweens are going to have definite ideas about what would be great in their space, and their ideas need to be integrated as much as is practical. With that said, signage is still huge. Make sure to invest a little money in signage that labels a particular area as "tween" and clearly indicates the tween shelves. That could take the form of different types of end-cap labels for the shelves or dividers for the shelves. Make it easy for tweens and their parents to know where the tween section is and find what they are looking for.

As far as decorating the tween area, do not spend money on decorations. Instead, let the tweens (most likely the tween advisory board, assuming there is one) decorate the area. Buy blank canvases at a craft store. Let them paint and create. Remember that tweens want to be creative and have a positive impact on their environment. There will be so much more positive feedback and feelings from tweens if they have as much control over their space as possible.

Good luck with the space. Remember, a lot can be done with elbow grease and determination. Money is great, but a big impact on the tweens can come from simply giving them their own materials separate from other people's, no matter what else happens.

The Takeaway

- Consider the positives and negatives of locating the tween space adjacent to either the children's materials or the young adult materials.
- Consider all potential elements of the tween collection to see if they need to be located together or kept where they currently are.
- Consider whether the new tween space can be decorated and if there are additional monetary resources to use for other things.

12

Finding Tween Materials
Within Collections

As with defining tweens themselves, defining tween materials may be more about what the materials are not instead of what they are. Bear in mind that since there is not a whole lot written about tweens, especially from more definitive sources, these guidelines must be viewed with an eye to the community as a whole.

In anecdotal discussions with staff from various libraries, it is not unusual to recount conversations with parents about the location of various materials. Parents can feel quite strongly about audiovisual materials in particular. A common conversation can be something like "Yes, we know that there are a number of families that let their 10-year-olds play *Call of Duty*, and some of those same families sit together and watch *The Walking Dead*. However, it does not appear that the community as a whole does that, so we are going to keep those items shelved with the other materials that have the same age recommendations as these." All youth librarians know that it is a balancing act to get materials in the best possible location.

The most important advice about preparing to develop a collection of tween materials is "read lots of books." In this case, read books at the upper end of the library's children's section, as well as selections from the library's young adult materials. Talk to the people who are ordering books for those sections. Borrow review journals from the collection development department (or whoever gets those magazines). Take a look at what the Association of Library Services to Children (ALSC) has listed for tween reads to get an idea of what might belong in the tween collection. As has been said before, creating a tween section of materials is not a decision to be made lightly. The investment of time and research at the beginning of the process will save a lot of headaches and redoing in the end.

Take a look at what characterizes the books in the children's section and those in the young adult section. What patterns are starting to emerge? Admittedly, if the youth fiction is separated into genres, it can make spotting trends easier, but that is not necessarily the case. It may be best to look at some different questions to ask as tween materials develop their own criteria and definition.

Who in the library is doing youth collection development? It is best to not make the decisions about tween books in a vacuum. Currently someone (or perhaps a group of people) in the library has been getting books for tweens even though they were not officially labeled as tween materials. Plan on working with these people to develop guidelines for tween books and eventually pull the books off the shelves and put them in a new section.

What Are the Differences Between Chapter Books?

This is not a question specifically about tween books, but it highlights some of the guidelines that will be covered later. Technically *Henry & Mudge* by Cynthia Rylant is a chapter book. Does that belong in the tween section? Probably not. Does *The Fault in Our Stars* by John Greene belong in the tween section? Again, probably not. It is really easy to say, "All chapter books belong in the tween section," but that category actually covers a wide range of territory in the overall youth fiction collection. It is possible to use a general number of pages to designate what is a tween chapter book versus a children's or young adult chapter book. However, for every "perfect-length" tween book, there will be a tween book that has 60 pages and another that has 500 pages. The *Harry Potter* books are a good example of books that defy a general page limit guideline.

If the Number of Pages Is Not Going to Be the Guide for Determining a Tween Book, What Else Can Be Used?

Looking at the youngest end of youth fiction, tween books are not board books or picture books. While there can be a reasonable argument made that there are picture books being published that are usable for tweens, that same argument can be made for picture books that work wonderfully well in adult storytimes at adult care facilities. However, do not forget that there are a tremendous number of wonderful graphic novels written for tweens. Again, page length or even illustrations versus just text are not going to be good criteria. *What distinguishes a tween book from a children's book or a young adult book is the topic of the book.*

What Can Be Used as General Guidelines?

Book reviews may not be as useful as one might expect—for example, one review may say the book is perfect for six year olds, while another claims it's perfect for preschoolers. The same can happen for tween books. There is the chronological age of the reader to consider as well as their maturity level. And there is absolutely nothing wrong with having a tween community that tends to be a bit more mature than average or a bit less mature than average. It is what the community is. Embrace that. However, here are some questions, irreverent as they may be, that will help determine what makes a good tween book.

Is there kissing? If there is kissing, but it is the sweet, innocent, "Oops, someone moved and I kissed their ear and not their lips," then it is probably a tween book. If there is tongue and spit swapping, it is probably a young adult book.

Are people "rounding bases"? This is a euphemism that ultimately asks whether there will be sex in the book. Sex, heavy petting, and making out in a car are all things that will push the book into the young adult section.

What are the adults in the story like? Not all the adults have to be perfect and respectable. They can have flaws. However, adults in tween books generally are not so flawed that the main character has no one to depend on. *Harriet the Spy* is a classic example of a tween book where the adults are flawed, but the main character still has adults in her life who are there for her. There are quite a few young adult books where the protagonist has no adults available for support and either finds contemporaries to depend on or has to do every-thing on his or her own. That having been said, there are also books like *Hatchet*, which is definitely a tween book even though there are no dependable adults in the story. Science fiction and fantasy books can have nonexistent adults as well, so this is not a hard and fast rule.

Are the books dealing with sexuality, race, and other sensitive topics of the day? This is not to say that gender identification and questions about racism have no place in tween books. They absolutely do; however, such topics generally are not the main focus of the story in tween books, as they can be in young adult literature. Tween books must include relevant, current topics, but gen-erally it is how central these subjects are to the story that sets tween books apart from young adult materials, where dystopian fiction and "the problem novel" are common.

What do the book covers look like? While many like to say, "Don't judge a book by its cover," unfortunately, that philosophy is going to get a tween librarian in trouble. Tweens are absolutely judging every book by the cover art and how it is designed, which will ultimately affect whether the book gets checked out. So look at the covers. Are girls in super short skirts? Does the boy on the cover look like he just finished modeling for a Harlequin romance novel? These are clues that this book probably is not for tweens. But at the same time, is cover art too juvenile? If so, then that book is not going out of the library with a tween. No one wants to read a "baby book."

What is happening with nonfiction materials for tweens? The answer may be "nothing." Based on the school assignments that tweens are getting, is it nec-essary to have a separate section for tween nonfiction? Are tweens using a younger reading level for their projects, or are they gravitating toward adult nonfiction? The answers to these questions may be all over the place. Perhaps nonfiction will stay the same (whatever "same" is for the library). At least think about it because someone will ask about tween nonfiction if there is a tween fiction section.

Now perhaps there is something to start with when it comes to discerning tween books. To reduce some very serious discussions to a few sound bites, a general rule of thumb is that if the book has sex, drugs, and rock and roll, it will be a young adult book. If there is kissing but the opposite gender is still a bit icky, then it is a tween book.

Periodicals have not been mentioned anywhere yet, but some magazines or periodical comics might be appropriate for tweens. To evaluate the periodical comics, use the same guidelines provided for graphic novels (which will be discussed below). However, magazines will be evaluated based on content; is it the same type of content as in the approved tween books? Once again, absolutely judge the magazine by its cover. If it looks babyish, leave it in the children's area. If the cover has a pop culture celebrity on it, then it is probably a tween magazine. Unfortunately, there are not a lot of magazines for tweens besides *Tiger Beat* and similar publications, but for some libraries, magazines are still quite popular. This subject will be discussed in more detail in the magazine chapter.

Graphic novels generally can be evaluated like a book when considering the elements of the storyline, but because they are visual, they are a little bit like AV materials as well, because when there is an actual picture to go with a story point instead of the reader using his or her imagination, evaluation requires a bit more thought. Consider the following questions.

What Is the Written Content Like?

Written content is the first thing to look at for graphic novels and manga. Does the storyline stay within what is considered acceptable according to the general tween book guidelines? Is it sweetly romantic instead of having a sex scene? Does it feature action and adventure without copious amounts of death or violence? In other words, "If the illustrations were removed, does it read like other tween books?" A word of caution as you go through the youth collection: Several Marvel and DC superheroes have graphic novels written for different audiences, but some libraries have them all shelved together. Many of these superheroes will need to have each of their subseries evaluated independently to see whether they belong in the tween collection or the young adult collection.

How Are Images Characterized in the Graphic Novel?

The reason why it is easier to look at the written content first is that sometimes it is right on the border of tween and young adult. However, it is the images accompanying the narrative that will ultimately tip the scale to either tween or young adult material. Generally the main characters in tween books, whether human or anthropomorphous animals or objects, are more stylized and cartoonish. These characters tend to be drawn with more rounded lines. They may appear cutesy instead of realistic. By contrast, the main characters in young adult graphic novels are more angular and in general anatomically correct, or else they may have an accentuated part of their anatomy, usually in the chest area, either overly muscular or overly large breasted. These characters tend to be drawn with more lines than curves. The color palette for a tween graphic novel tends to be bright colors; these can be primary, pastel, or florescent, but they are bright, and overall the images are full of light. By contrast, the color palette of a young adult graphic novel is muted and darker, and there is a lot of shading and shadowing. Generally the colors are browns, grays, blacks, blues, and purples. Reds, yellows, and whites are accent colors that leap off the page in contrast to the rest of the images.

How Are Images Characterized in Manga?

Manga can be a challenge separate from but related to American graphic novels. Sometimes ratings on the back of the book can help with deciding what section of the library manga belongs in. However, publishers do not have a consistent rating system, and some manga may not have a rating at all. Sometimes a series of manga changes from a rating considered acceptable for tweens to one that is definitely suggesting the content is for young adults. Since manga as a style of drawing features exaggerated body features, evaluating it for age appropriateness can be more of a challenge. Most of the characters for all reading levels appear cutesy. However, if the main characters are not human, there is a decent chance that the books are appropriate for tweens. Generally in young adult manga all the characters are human or human-like. For manga, determining appropriateness will depend a bit more heavily on the narrative itself. What situations are the characters facing? Is the opposite gender icky, or is sex a definite possibility? When looking at the images, check how much clothing characters are wearing, particularly female characters. Put simply, if the skirts are super short and there is cleavage showing, then that manga stays in the young adult area.

However, everything changes again when evaluating tween media. This area comes with a different set of challenges to deal with, and it can be very discussion laden as far as what music or movies are appropriate for tweens. Look to the community, as they are going to indicate what is appropriate for children. It is not something to ask overtly, but by talking to tweens about what they watch or listen to, librarians can get a sense of what is going to be a good fit. Ideas will also come from watching what parents of tweens check out of the library. However, there are once again certain guidelines to use.

What Can Go in a Tween Movie Section?

Guidelines will most likely already be in place for deciding what DVDs/Blu-rays belong in the children's section; whatever is not a children's DVD/Blu-ray is probably going to be for tweens. For a long time in many libraries, the suggested guideline was that only G movies belong in the children's section, and the television ratings were either Y or Y7. That worked until some of the Disney animated films that everyone saw were rated PG. So now children's DVDs/Blu-rays will include mostly G-rated movies with a few popular PG movies thrown in. Many older television shows for children are unrated, but most of the time someone on the staff will have seen the show and can provide advice.

Originally the guideline for tween movies was PG-rated movies only and the seasons of television shows that played on Disney, Nickelodeon, and other channels but were definitely marketed to tweens. Generally the television shows were rated PG (if they were rated at all). However, some of the Harry Potter movies and a handful of other movies made from tween books earned PG-13 ratings. Lately, the tween DVD/Blu-ray section for most libraries has become quite a mixture of items. G-rated Disney movies that are more popular with tween grandparents than anyone else are sharing shelf space with *Harry Potter*, *Pirates of the Caribbean*, an episode of *Austin & Ally*, and the various seasons of *Boy Meets World* from the 1990s. The movies from the Marvel franchise that Disney has made present an interesting challenge because they illustrate the importance of understanding what is appropriate for the community. These movies are all rated PG-13; however, many of the youngest tweens will have seen these movies in the theater with their families. Knowing that, is it appropriate, or expected, to get copies of these movies for the tween AV section?

What Tween Video Games Does the Library Have?

Tween video games are fairly similar to DVDs and Blu-rays because they are highly visual. Also, like movies and television shows, video games have ratings (and in this case every video game comes with a rating). As a general rule, E10 games should go to tweens. However, there are many E titles that appeal to tweens, but because everyone can play E-rated games together regardless of age, these games may be shelved somewhere else. If the library is able to purchase multiple copies of video games, then some copies can go in the children's area and others in the tween area—that is the best of both worlds.

What About Tween Music?

These days many tweens obtain their music from an online media service like iTunes or Amazon Prime, so building a tween music collection in the library may be a low priority. However, things like soundtracks for the films in the tween movie collection are good choices for a tween CD collection, as well as music from artists featured on tween-focused television shows and movies. The content thresholds used for books and movies apply to music as well. For example, are the topics covered in the lyrics appropriate for tweens? Unfortunately, if a popular tween television star puts out an album where every other word is a swear word, then that CD is probably not going to belong in the tween music collection.

What About Books on CD or Playaways?

If the print copy of a book is in the tween section, then the corresponding book on CD or Playaway should be in the tween collection as well.

What About Library Streaming Services?
Do They Get Marketed to Tweens?

It is an individual library's decision to subscribe to Hoopla, Freegal, Overdrive, Zinio, 3M, or any number of other services that provide access to music, movies, ebooks, and magazines. There are titles available within these services that will appeal to tweens. Since these are services and not materials that take up physical space in the library, subscribing may not be something to consider right away, but be aware of what (if anything) these services offer that might fit within the existing guidelines for tweens. Does the library want to market the services to tweens when marketing the entire tween space? Also, make sure that the parents are aware that through these services their tweens could access a lot of adult material and it is not a specifically tween library service.

Having established an idea of what print and media offerings should be part of the tween section, it is best to move on to what particular materials might belong there. However, remember to really take a look at the community to see what fits best. Please ask some actual tweens; they will be the best indicators of what will be appropriate for your library.

The Takeaway

Tween materials should:

- reflect the maturity level of the community's tweens, being neither too childish nor too mature in content;
- represent community-appropriate books, magazines, graphic novels, and audiovisual materials; and
- offer tweens many different options of materials to borrow, demonstrating that time, effort, and care have gone into creating the tween collection.

SECTION V

Tween Materials

This section covers a wide variety of tween-appropriate materials. These are suggestions, and by no means an exhaustive list of everything necessary for a tween collection.

In the first chapter, there is a lengthy list of books that could be in a tween collection. However, the focus is on potential genres of books (and examples thereof). Use this guide to go through the library's existing youth materials collection to find titles that can quickly be marked and moved to the tween collection. This list is intended to spark thoughts of book possibilities already in the library. However, if there is something on this list that the library does not have, the titles should be available through most library book vendors.

The second chapter is specifically about helping out the reluctant reader. Connecting with and helping a reluctant reader find something to read and be successful with is what being a tween librarian is all about. It can sometimes seem that tweens have a higher percentage of reluctant readers, but perhaps they are just more noticeable at this age.

There is also a short chapter on magazines for tweens—short because there are not many tween-focused magazines to talk about. However, some libraries have successful and large circulations of magazines. Therefore, it is necessary to discuss examples of appropriate titles for tweens.

The final chapter is about audiovisual materials for tweens—DVDs (and/or Blurays), CDs, and video games. There is a lot out there, and much time and money can be spent creating the perfect tween AV section. However, as with books, possible material may already be present in other locations in the library.

It bears repeating once again that tween collections are very community dependent. Not all of these suggestions will work in every library. There is no "Perfect List of Tween Materials." If nothing else, use this as a list of suggested materials to help "get to know" tween literature.

13

An Annotated Sample List of Tween Books

There are many amazing books for tweens available, and what follows is by no means an exhaustive list. It may even appear like it is a list without a tremendous amount of variety. This chapter touches on some newer books as well as some older books, and if a book is part of a series, it is the series that is listed, not the individual titles. An attempt has been made to ensure that these books are still in print and can be purchased. As a result, there may be some interesting tween books or series left off this list solely because they are no longer in print. Each annotation is more like the explanation of why that selection is an awesome tween book, not necessarily a plot summary of the book or series. Of course, remember that a tween librarian knows his or her community best.

The books are separated into genres, so as to make sure this list is not weighted too much to any particular type of book (although the next chapter talks specifically about good books for reluctant tween readers). Within genres, a lot of the books are (unsurprisingly) very similar. When an author or publisher finds a successful plot, set of characters, or combination of narrative elements, there are going to be a large number of similar books. That's okay. Many tweens find one thing they like and want only things that are like that. While librarians try to have a balanced collection with many different books and ideas to appeal to different people, sometimes it just makes sense to get books that are going to be really popular in the community regardless of whether the book in question is basically the same as something else.

Having fiction divided into genres can be very helpful for readers trying to find something, anything, that they like. It can also be helpful for parents who need to find something "just like" this other book that their tweens have read. Sometimes the challenge is that an author may write in multiple genres, so that the author's body of work is split into different locations. Deciding whether the library values the genre more or prefers to keep the author's body of work together is a very personal decision and specific to the community. However, splitting the collection into genres can also bring up discussions of why there is not this or that genre. For example, there is not a specific section in this chapter for inspirational fiction (which is not to say that there are not a lot of great tween books in this genre). There is not a section for sports stories, either; they are in a broader genre. There is a genre called "Classics" that includes both award-winning books and books of lasting interest. However, not all the "old books" are classics. Sometimes they are kept in their appropriate genre (and some books could potentially belong to more than one genre).

Putting books in genres is an ever evolving process. Such categorization can reflect current community interests as well as larger popular culture ideas. Sometimes one genre loses popularity over time while another rises to prominence. Librarians are constantly adding and removing items from collections. One library may choose to have a separate collection of Newbery Award winners, and a neighboring library may choose to have both Newbery winners and honor books shelved separately. If a community is heavily involved in its state's book award, the librarians may want to keep those books separate. Getting input from the community members about what genres they prefer or would like to see gathered together can help quite a bit in the long run.

Series books for tweens are emphasized here. Finding one book in a series and sticking with it tends to appeal to a lot of tweens. Any reading is good reading, whether it is a cereal box, recipe directions, a classic novel, or a compilation of facts. Some books do not have lasting literary merit, but they are lovely pieces of escapist, light reading. For tweens who teeter on the brink of "reading is cool" and "reading is absolutely horrible," it is imperative to validate their reading choices, whatever they are. Lifelong readers is what librarians want. What tweens read sometimes does not matter as much!

Action

This could also be called Adventure or even Action/Adventure. Almost all the books involve children or teens facing some challenge without the help of adults (or even in spite of adults). Facing either a defined evil or simply the challenge of survival, there is something romantic or aspirational about these books. It's easy for tweens to imagine what they would do in these situations and how they would triumph in the end.

39 CLUES. NEW YORK: SCHOLASTIC

Four series exist within the *39 Clues* world: the original *39 Clues* stories (also referred to in some places as *The Clue Hunt*) as well as *Cahills vs. Vespers, Unstoppable,* and *Doublecross.* What makes these books good tween options is that they feature lots of action and adventure. This is also a series to be read in order, and it is continuing to grow. In addition, since many schools do Scholastic Book Fairs, doing something along the lines of "The book fair can only have some of the *39 Clues* books, but the public library has them all!" can be a nice school and library tie-in. Obviously the idea is not to be antagonistic, but marketing and appealing to tweens is always helpful. This series works well in a marketing sense. And if the marketing possibilities did not make these books awesome enough, they are written by different authors, so librarians have the opportunity to say, "If you liked this book written by _____, then you might also like these other books he/she wrote."

GUTMAN, DAN. *GENIUS FILES*. NEW YORK: HARPERCOLLINS

Dan Gutman's books are both humorous and adventurous. If humor can be combined with any other genre, it is a pretty sure bet for success with tweens. Gutman has a history of solid tween-popular titles, and this series is no exception. Individual librarians can decide what genre classification works best.

HOROWITZ, ANTHONY. *ALEX RIDER*. NEW YORK: PHILOMEL BOOKS

This series is also going to appeal to the older tweens. Depending on the community, this might be a young adult series. Additionally, the first book was made into a movie. The opportunity to offer a tween a book and its movie (regardless of whether it is a good movie) tends to give the book and its subsequent series members some extra cachet for many tweens. There are also a few graphic novels for this series. Again, when a book is presented in multiple ways, it becomes "cooler" for many tweens.

HOROWITZ, ANTHONY. *GATEKEEPERS*. NEW YORK: SCHOLASTIC

This series is geared toward the older end of the tween spectrum. It could also be put in the fantasy genre if that would work better in the library. Anthony Horowitz has great appeal as an author since he tends to write fast-paced books. These five books need to be read in order and are best for tweens who perhaps like (or think they like) horror or scary books.

INFINITY RING. NEW YORK: SCHOLASTIC

Just about all the things said about *39 Clues* apply here as well. There's nothing wrong with finding a successful formula and repeating it. That is what Scholastic has done with another series authored by multiple people. This series features adventure with a definite science fiction bent. Time travel is a fun topic, so this could appeal to many different types of tweens.

MONNINGER, JOSEPH. *STAY ALIVE*. NEW YORK: SCHOLASTIC

This is a paperback series, which may or may not make a difference in the library (depending on whether paperbacks are shelved separately). This series would be something to recommend to tweens who like *Hatchet* by Gary Paulsen. The books are about a group of children who have to survive after adults are not able to help or care for them.

PATTERSON, JAMES. *TREASURE HUNTERS*. NEW YORK: LITTLE, BROWN

This series has some similarities to Dan Gutman's *Genius Files* as far as siblings having adventures in different places. Certainly James Patterson is a prolific author, and he co-authors many series with other writers, including this series co-written with Chris Gravenstein. These books could also be in a humorous genre.

PROBST, JEFF. *STRANDED*. NEW YORK: PUFFIN BOOKS

While the plot for this series sounds like many of the other action books in this collection, it deserves a special mention because the author is a television personality. Tweens are so plugged into television and popular culture that something even remotely tied to television or movies can be extremely popular. Don't brush off this series because it might not be as high quality as is generally preferred. Showing tweens that their librarian is aware of what is going on outside the library walls can be quite beneficial.

SNICKET, LEMONY. *A SERIES OF UNFORTUNATE EVENTS*. NEW YORK: HARPERCOLLINS

These books are perennial favorites with tweens. There is something wonderful about reading about other people's horrible lives and then thinking that maybe yours definitely is not so bad. Of course, this series also has a big-budget movie that goes along with some of the volumes. The books also tend to have the cachet of "my older brother/sister/cousin/neighbor loved them, so now I'm going to read them."

STEWART, TRENTON LEE. *MYSTERIOUS BENEDICT SOCIETY*. NEW YORK: LITTLE, BROWN BOOKS FOR YOUNG READERS

Potentially a short mystery series instead of adventure, this series has all the intrigue, horrible adults, and children capable of saving the world that any tween could want. This is what makes it more adventure-like.

Fantasy

Fantasy has become one of the most popular genres since the publication of the *Harry Potter* books and subsequent novels about wizards and other fantastical elements. And with the popularity of television shows like *Once Upon a Time* and *Grimm*, there seems to be a subset of fantasy books that focus more on the folktale and fairy tale elements of fantasy. Sometimes these are funny and sometimes they combine other genres into the story, like mystery or even a bit of romance. However, these are different from the stories that seem to fit a more traditional definition of fantasy. Separating fantasy into subgenres may appear to give it more weight than other areas, but since Harry Potter has become such a cultural phenomenon, this genre still has quite a bit of staying power and popularity!

Light Fantasy

BAKER, E.D. *TALES OF THE FROG PRINCESS.* NEW YORK: BLOOMSBURY

This series of books plays with and expands the fairy tale "The Frog Prince." These titles appeal mostly to tween girls. Whether they wish they could be a princess or love the sweet romantic elements within the series, they are good examples of lighter fantasy books.

BARRY, DAVE. *STARCATCHERS.* NEW YORK: HYPERION

Co-writer Ridley Pearson has other tween fantasy offerings. This series expands on the story of Peter Pan. Since *Peter Pan* can be a popular local theater production, these books may have added tween appeal.

BUCKLEY, MICHAEL. *SISTERS GRIMM.* NEW YORK: AMULET BOOKS

This could belong in the mystery genre, but with the stories connecting back to the Brothers Grimm, the series may have more appeal for those tweens who read fairy tales and folktales. The sisters follow the trope of tweens without parents surviving and thriving amid evil in the world.

COWELL, CRESSIDA. *HOW TO TRAIN YOUR DRAGON.* NEW YORK:
   LITTLE, BROWN BOOKS FOR YOUNG READERS

This book series is also a successful movie franchise. There are lots of ways to convince tweens to read these books. Whenever there is a movie to complement the books, it is easier to pitch, especially to reluctant reader tweens.

GIDWITZ, ADAM. *GRIMM.* NEW YORK: DUTTON

This trilogy combines fantasy, humor, and folklore into a narrative similar to *A Series of Unfortunate Events*. It is easy to recommend this trio of books for tweens. However, quite a few adults read them as well!

HOLUB, JOAN. *GODDESS GIRLS.* NEW YORK: ALADDIN PAPERBACKS

This series will appeal primarily to tween girls. Were it not for Greek mythology that appears throughout these books, they could be categorized in the realistic fiction genre.

HOLUB, JOAN. *GRIMMTASTIC GIRLS.* NEW YORK: SCHOLASTIC

Similar to Holub's other series, *Goddess Girls*, this paperback series reads more like a realistic fiction series for tween girls except that there are elements of classic fairy tales playing major roles in the plots. This could also be described as "chick lit."

KRULIK, NANCY E. *KATIE KAZOO, SWITCHEROO*. NEW YORK:
GROSSET & DUNLAP

This series for young tweens tells quick and entertaining stories about a girl who switches places with different people. Technically this is a fantasy book, although it doesn't appear at first to have much in common with the more traditional types of stories.

LEVINE, GAIL CARSON. *ELLA ENCHANTED*. NEW YORK: HARPERCOLLINS

In addition to being a Newbery Honor book, *Ella Enchanted* was made into a Disney movie; thus, this book has a lot of tween appeal even though it was published long before the current tweens were born. Despite its age, the story is still enjoyable and a good option to offer tweens interested in unconventional princess stories.

PEARSON, RIDLEY. *KINGDOM KEEPERS*. NEW YORK: HYPERION

It's an interesting premise to have Disney villains appear throughout this series, which could also fit within the mystery genre. The fantasy elements fit well with the fantastic nature of the Disney theme parks in general and could be recommended to tweens who have just gone to or are planning to visit Disney attractions.

Traditional Fantasy

COLFER, EOIN. *ARTEMIS FOWL*. NEW YORK: HYPERION BOOKS
FOR CHILDREN

While Artemis Fowl is not a traditional hero, he is the main character in a compelling series of fantasy books for tweens. He remains popular since he is a criminal mastermind navigating various challenges in the different books.

DITERLIZZI, TONY. *SPIDERWICK*. NEW YORK: SIMON & SCHUSTER
CHILDREN'S PUBLISHING

Co-authored with Holly Black, a popular young adult author in her own right, two series—*Spiderwick Chronicles* and *Beyond the Spiderwick Chronicles*—hold tweens' attention with different adventures throughout all the books.

DUPRAU, JEANNE. *BOOK OF EMBER*. NEW YORK: RANDOM HOUSE BOOKS
FOR YOUNG READERS

It's another series with a movie attached. Regardless of whether people like the movies as much as the books, book/movie combos work well for tweens.

FLANAGAN, JOHN. *RANGER'S APPRENTICE*. NEW YORK: PHILOMEL

A fantasy/adventure series, these books can also appeal to historical fiction–minded tweens. It is written in the tradition of many other popular tween fantasy series.

FUNK, CORNELIA. *INKHEART*. NEW YORK: CHICKEN HOUSE

Again, it is a book/movie combination. Those are always worth promoting to tweens.

JACQUES, BRIAN. *REDWALL*. NEW YORK: PHILOMEL

This series, which features animals as the main characters, shares some similarities with many of the classic fantasy series for children. It is also a good series to recommend to the rabid fans of Erin Hunter's *Warriors*, *Seekers*, and *Survivors* books.

PATTERSON, JAMES. *WITCH & WIZARD*. NEW YORK: LITTLE, BROWN

This series is going to be for older tweens, and, depending on the community, it may actually be a young adult title. Since it is a bit dystopian in nature, it may be necessary to think carefully about whether this is right for the tween collection. However, it is a popular read with tweens.

PULLMAN, PHILLIP. *HIS DARK MATERIALS*. NEW YORK:
ALFRED A. KNOPF

This trilogy also contains its fair share of darkness, and it may not be right for every community's tweens. It has been available for a while. There is also a movie that accompanies the first book in the series, so, again, it is impossible to pass up the book/movie combination.

RIORDAN, RICK. *PERCY JACKSON*. NEW YORK: HYPERION

Rick Riordan has written both the *Percy Jackson and the Olympians* books and the related series *Heroes of Olympus*. There are also two Percy Jackson movies. The other interesting thing about these books is that quite a few parents and tweens read them together. There were many parents who really got into the series, perhaps even more than their children.

ROWLING, J.K. *HARRY POTTER*. NEW YORK: SCHOLASTIC

There is not much that needs to be said about this series. Even though the books mature and get darker as Harry gets older, they are still great reads for tweens. Of course, there are movies for each book as well.

Classics

It goes without saying that books that win the Newbery Medal will probably be classics. Most of the Newbery books tend to be tween titles. This list does not call attention to books that won Newbery Medals specifically, since most librarians already know about them. Many of the classics listed here have been published and republished many times. The citations provide only the author and the title of the books or series.

ALEXANDER, LLOYD. *CHRONICLES OF PRYDAIN*

There is a Disney movie that was made from one of these books, and there is a Newbery winner in the series as well. However, this series can sometimes escape tweens' notice because it may not be packaged as slickly as more contemporary publications. It has a lasting fantasy storyline, so it is worth reminding tweens that it is around. It is probably a parent or grandparent favorite.

BAUM, L. FRANK. *OZ*

Any and all of the *Wizard of Oz* stories are good reads for tweens. Many tweens may not even be aware that the classic movie was inspired by a series of books that were around long before Judy Garland or any other subsequent movie adaptations.

CARROLL, LEWIS. *ALICE'S ADVENTURES IN WONDERLAND*

This book and its sequel *Through the Looking Glass* are good titles to recommend to tweens, especially with the many different versions of the Alice story that have been made into movies. This is also a perennial adult favorite.

COOPER, SUSAN. *THE DARK IS RISING*

One of the books in this series won the Newbery Medal, but the entire series is worth recommending for tweens. Again, it can suffer from not having the attractive packaging of other books, but it is a great fantasy series.

DAHL, ROALD. *CHARLIE AND THE CHOCOLATE FACTORY*

Picking just one Roald Dahl book to mention is practically impossible. While *Charlie and the Chocolate Factory* has been made into multiple movies (always a good selling point for tweens), just about all of the Roald Dahl books for children are appropriate tween reads. The humor and attitudes toward adults fit well with the tween mindset.

FARLEY, WALTER. *BLACK STALLION*

This is another series that may be good to have in the tween section for tweens' parents and grandparents. They are great horse stories, but sometimes it is equally rewarding to help generations talk with each other about books they love.

LEWIS, C.S. *CHRONICLES OF NARNIA*

There are several fairly current movies based on the Narnia books. Many tweens' parents and grandparents grew up reading these books and may even have fond memories of earlier adaptations of the stories. Some tweens do not realize that these were books before they were movies.

MONTGOMERY, L.M. *ANNE OF GREEN GABLES*

This series seems to continue as a perennial favorite of tween girls as well as their mothers and grandmothers. While the stories in the series follow Anne through childhood into adulthood and motherhood, the books are sweetly romantic and generally even the later titles would still be fine for older tweens. However, this may be something to consider for the community. Is it necessary to split the series into two different areas based on Anne's maturation?

PACKARD, EDWARD. *CHOOSE YOUR OWN ADVENTURES*

Parents of tweens will remember these staples of their childhood, many of which have been reprinted as of late. There is still something wonderful about these books. They are also a great choice to offer to parents of reluctant readers. While their children may not want to read these books, it can help these reluctant readers to see their parents light up with great memories of a fun book.

WILDER, LAURA INGALLS. *LITTLE HOUSE ON THE PRAIRIE*

Many tweens' parents or even grandparents watched the television show based on the *Little House* books, and even though the books are probably best for young tweens, they are worth mentioning. Some libraries have companion volumes that are spun-off series about other characters within "Laura's World."

Fiction

This can be simply contemporary fiction, or it can be the catch-all category for books that do not seem to fit somewhere else. It can even be the place where smaller genres are located because there are not enough of them to have their own section in the tween book area. There are subsets of fiction that seem like they could become their own genre, but perhaps the library is not quite ready to label them that way. Among other things, there are a number of books that cater specifically to tween girls. These books will be treated separately from the rest of the fiction collection, and they will be called "chick lit" (like their adult counterparts).

General Fiction

CHRISTOPHER, MATT

Here is a tween author known for many different sports stories. His books are on quintessential tween topics and written to appeal to this group. Some libraries may find that sports is a good genre in itself instead of placing these stories in a general category.

CREECH, SHARON. *LOVE THAT DOG*. NEW YORK: JOANNA COTLER BOOKS

This book serves as a reminder for librarians that novels in verse can be good choices for tweens. This is a fun book, and it has the appearance of being much longer than it really is, making it a good reluctant reader book as well.

DAVIES, JACQUELINE. *LEMONADE WARS*. BOSTON: HOUGHTON MIFFLIN

Sometimes the individual books in this series seem like they might belong in a genre other than general fiction, thus illustrating the usefulness of having the "fiction" category as a catch-all location for individual books or series that seem to fit in multiple places. However, overall *Lemonade Wars* is a great tween series, regardless of its location in the library.

HAPKA, CATHERINE. *HORSE DIARIES*. NEW YORK: RANDOM HOUSE
   BOOKS FOR YOUNG READERS

Horses and dogs seem to be popular with tweens. There are a number of great contemporary and classic horse series; this is just one that has been popular lately. Horses may not be as popular in some areas, but is there another really popular animal?

KLIMO, KATE. *DOG DIARIES*. NEW YORK: RANDOM HOUSE BOOKS
   FOR YOUNG READERS

This paperback series serves as a great reminder that paperbacks can be popular with tweens. As mentioned before, there are also a lot of great books about animals. Whether there is a separate animal genre or not, tweens love reading about their favorite animals.

KORMAN, GORDON. *SWINDLE*. NEW YORK: SCHOLASTIC

Gordon Korman in general is a tween author. Arguably his *Swindle* series could belong in the humorous genre (if such a genre exists in the library), but all of Korman's books should be in the tween collection.

LUPICA, MIKE

Mike Lupica has written quite a few great tween sports series. *Comeback Kids* and *Game Changers* are two favorites. He is good to recommend to Matt Christopher fans as well.

LYNCH, CHRIS. *VIETNAM*. NEW YORK: SCHOLASTIC

Vietnam could be an older tween series. It is arguably a historical fiction series as well; however, sometimes a genre label of "historical fiction" can be a death knell for a book or series if historical fiction is deemed "uncool" by the tweens. For young patrons who are aware of the wars going on around the world or those whose families are touched by military service, this is a good series to recommend.

LYNCH, CHRIS. *WORLD WAR II.* NEW YORK: SCHOLASTIC

Basically the same ideas from *Vietnam* apply here as well. Again, nothing wrong with staying with a formula that works.

SELZNICK, BRIAN. *WONDERSTRUCK.* NEW YORK: SCHOLASTIC

Another genre-bending tween book with a great story. There is something pretty fabulous about seeing a tween carrying around this really chunky book.

Chick Lit

BENTON, JIM. *DEAR DUMB DIARY.* NEW YORK: SCHOLASTIC PAPERBACKS

This book arguably could be in the humorous section, if such exists, as it is a funny take on a tween girl's life. It also comes with a sequel: *Dear Dumb Diary Year Two.*

DEVILLERS, JULIA

Most of Julia DeVillers' books are standalone titles, and she excels at writing the tween girl story. Since some of her books were published almost ten years ago, there may be copies in another part of the collection that could be moved to the tween section.

FREDERICK, HEATHER VOGEL. *MOTHER-DAUGHTER BOOK CLUB.* NEW YORK: SIMON & SCHUSTER BOOKS FOR YOUNG READERS

These are fun, light books for tweens, and, as a bonus, this series introduces a classic book to tween readers. This can also inspire tweens or their librarians to want to try establishing a mother-daughter book club themselves.

HAN, JENNY. *SHUG.* NEW YORK: SIMON & SCHUSTER'S CHILDREN'S PUBLISHING

While Jenny Han is known more as a young adult author, this book is definitely a tween title. It is always good to be able to say to a tween who is ready to read more mature young adult titles that she has already read and liked something by that same author.

IGNATOW, AMY. *POPULARITY PAPERS.* NEW YORK: AMULET BOOKS

This series features two endearing girl heroines. The middle school crises they experience are genuine and, as adults, absolutely hilarious. Written in an approachable style, this is a slightly more mature version of the *Amelia's Diary* books that were quite popular a few years ago.

MASS, WENDY. *WILLOW FALLS.* NEW YORK: SCHOLASTIC PRESS

Perhaps these titles belong more with fantasy books, but the series does have more of a chick lit element to it. It is a great series of tween books.

MORGAN, MELISSA J. *CAMP CONFIDENTIAL.* NEW YORK: GROSSET & DUNLAP

This paperback series focuses on the romantic notion of summer camp and the adventures that can be had there. It's a fun choice for tweens and probably one that is already somewhere in the library.

MYRACLE, LAUREN

While her *Internet Girls* series is intended for young adults, Lauren Myracle does have two enjoyable tween chick lit series: the *Winnie Years* and the *Flower Power* quartet. Unfortunately, there is no boy appeal here.

SIMON, COCO. *CUPCAKE DIARIES.* NEW YORK: SIMON SPOTLIGHT

This series capitalizes on the current craze with cooking and all things culinary. This trend has not escaped tweens' notice, since they are plugged into popular culture.

WEEKS, SARAH. *PIE.* NEW YORK: SCHOLASTIC

While Sarah Weeks writes many different books for a variety of age levels, this is great young tween book that involves a bit of mystery, but mostly it is about family and other things that tweens can relate to.

Graphic Novels

There is quite an extensive list of graphic novels in the following chapter, which focuses specifically on books for reluctant readers. However, the graphic novels mentioned below are either historical or semi-autobiographical in nature. While reluctant readers may enjoy them very much, they have a different tone from the graphic novels discussed elsewhere.

ABIRACHED, ZEINA. *A GAME FOR SWALLOWS: TO DIE, TO LEAVE, TO RETURN.* NEW YORK: GRAPHIC UNIVERSE

This is a true story, and a very serious one at that. Even though it is a quick read, and from the cover it looks like it could be read by young tweens, the subject matter is definitely for older kids. This book is good to recommend to parents of tweens because it definitely blows away the stereotype of what graphic novels are.

ABIRACHED, ZEINA. *I REMEMBER BEIRUT.* NEW YORK:
  GRAPHIC UNIVERSE

This is basically the next chapter in Zeina's story. The reasons to recommend it are the same as the first book. It is best to read these books in order, but it is not absolutely necessary.

BELL, CECE. *EL DEAFO.* NEW YORK: AMULET BOOKS

This graphic novel is semi-autobiographical, and it is a quick read for tweens who are feeling different. This works well as a school book-talk subject because a chunk of the action happens in a school.

LEWIS, JOHN. *MARCH: BOOK ONE.* MARIETTA: TOP SHELF

While this could be a tougher sell to older tweens on their own, this is a graphic novel best pitched to parents and teachers of tweens. Remember, the books must be read in order!

LEWIS, JOHN. *MARCH: BOOK TWO.* MARIETTA: TOP SHELF

This is the second in the series. These books cannot be read out of order, or the story will not make sense. Again, use these books more with adults who work with tweens.

YANG, GENE LUEN. *AMERICAN BORN CHINESE.* NEW YORK:
  SQUARE FISH

As a book geared toward older tweens, this graphic novel may end up in the young adult section, depending on the community. It probably needs a book talk or a personal sell to many tweens, but it is definitely worth the effort.

YANG, GENE LUEN. *LEVEL UP.* NEW YORK: FIRST SECOND

This is definitely an older tween book, and potentially, depending on the community, it may belong in the teen or young adult collection. However, it works well as a book to begin a discussion about cultures or different family dynamics.

Humorous Books

As with graphic novels, there is an extensive list of humorous books included in the reluctant reader chapter. However, the books listed here are going to be older. Because of that, simply the author and title of the book/series are listed. Perhaps a good way to think about this group is "classic humor"?

BLUME, JUDY. *ARE YOU THERE GOD? IT'S ME, MARGARET*

A classic book for tween girls, it can be controversial as well as nostalgic. However, it is something that is still funny today and a book that mothers and daughters can read together.

BLUME, JUDY. *FUDGE*

The Fudge books include *Tales of a Fourth Grade Nothing*, *Superfudge*, *Fudge-a-mania*, and *Double Fudge*. These have been favorites of young tweens for many years because they can all relate to Peter Hatcher and his brother Fudge.

CLEARY, BEVERLY. *HENRY HUGGINS*

These classic stories about Henry, his neighbors, and his dog, Ribsy, will definitely appeal more to the young end of the tween spectrum. However, these books are classics that can be read by tweens and their parents and grandparents.

MACDONALD, BETTY. *MRS. PIGGLE-WIGGLE*

While some parts of this series may feel dated for contemporary tweens, there is something to be said for the nostalgia value it brings to tweens' parents and grandparents. When an adult wants a "classic" for tweens, these are books they will read and enjoy.

SACHAR, LOUIS. *WAYSIDE SCHOOL*

There are three books in this series: *Sideways Stories from Wayside School*, *Wayside School Is Falling Down*, and *Wayside School Gets a Little Stranger*. These are on the young end of tween books, but they have remained popular with reluctant and competent readers alike.

ROCKWELL, THOMAS. *HOW TO EAT FRIED WORMS*

There is something wonderful about the staying power of eating worms. While this is a younger tween book, it will also get a good response from older tweens and a nostalgic look from parents and even grandparents.

RODGERS, MARY. *FREAKY FRIDAY*

Freaky Friday works well for the book and movie combination sell. Even though the book has been out for quite a while, as well as the several movie adaptations, they remain enjoyable, particularly for young tweens.

Manga

There are many different manga series to choose from, most of which have their own age ratings on the back cover. Manga can be a touchy subject with certain people, including parents, teachers, and grandparents. Some feel the content is too mature for tweens, expressing concern that the cartoonish drawings may attract young children to subjects they should not be exposed to. Following the ratings that the publishers put on the back of the books is a good start for building the manga section of the tween collection. However, sometimes it is better to evaluate the series as a whole to decide whether the content is appropriate for tweens or belongs somewhere else. The age range for tweens in a particular community is going to be extremely important in this genre. A lot of the manga ratings are either T for Teen or 13+; that can be at the top end of the tween range, or it may be outside the community's tweens.

Manga is not for everyone; reading a book from right to left and back to front confuses many people. However, if the tweens enjoy the books, that is all that matters. The other interesting thing with manga is that it can be a genre that tweens read in order to appear like the teenagers who are reading more mature manga series. A challenge that comes with purchasing manga is that it seems to go in and out of print fairly quickly. An attempt has been made below to include books that are currently in print, but remember that there may be some of these books already in the library, so that they simply need to be moved to the tween area. Many of the manga series that are appropriate for tweens tend to be more focused on a girl audience, although that is not to say that some series would not appeal to both genders. However, the manga selections are divided into girl focused and gender neutral.

Girl Focused

CIBOS, LINDSAY. *PEACH FUZZ.* EDINA, MN: SPOTLIGHT

With a ferret and her owner, Amanda, as the focus of this trilogy, these books play on many tweens' desire to have a pet of their own. It is originally written in English, which makes it different from many of the manga that will be available for tweens.

HAKAMADA, MERA. *FAIRY IDOL KANON.* ONTARIO:
UDON ENTERTAINMENT

Kanon and friends are involved in different adventures. This series is very much in line with the "group of friends" books that are common tropes for tween girls.

KONAMI, KANATA. *CHI'S SWEET HOME.* NEW YORK: VERTICAL

These stories of a kitten's adventures will likely appeal more to girls even though the kitten lives with a young boy. While this could be a gender-neutral series, it appears that girls like and check out these books more often than boys.

SONODA, KONAMI. *CHOCOMIMI.* SAN FRANCISCO: VIZ MEDIA

Following the adventures of two tween girls, the bright colors and perky female characters make this a very girl-focused series.

TATSUYAMA, SAYURI. *HAPPY HAPPY CLOVER*. SAN FRANCISCO:
VIZ MEDIA

This series follows four bunnies on a variety of adventures. This series has been popular with the tweens who like *Chi's Sweet Home* and *Fluffy, Fluffy, Cinnamoroll*.

TSUKIRINO, YUMI. *FLUFFY, FLUFFY CINNAMOROLL*. SAN FRANCISCO:
VIZ MEDIA

It could be worth arguing that since the main character is a male dog with a cinnamon roll for a tail, this manga could be classed as "gender neutral," but it seems to be extremely popular with young tween girls.

TURNER, JAMES. *MAMESHIBA*. SAN FRANCISCO: VIZ MEDIA

Curious, cute, bean-shaped creatures are again more the province of tween girls. The facial expressions of many of the characters are reminiscent of numerous Pokémon characters.

Gender Neutral

AMANA, SHIRO. *KINGDOM HEARTS*. NEW YORK: YEN PRESS

There are many different subseries that fall under the *Kingdom Hearts* umbrella. Overall, this manga revolves around adventures that include Disney characters along with other personalities.

DE CAMPI, ALEX. *KAT & MOUSE*. EDINA, MN: SPOTLIGHT

The story in this series has a mystery slant. Kat is female and Mouse is male, and they go to the same private school. This type of schooling tends to be of interest to tweens, since most attend public schools.

HIMEKAWA, AKIRA. *LEGEND OF ZELDA*. SAN FRANCISCO: VIZ MEDIA

This is going to be a great recommendation for video game–loving tweens. It is a good way to tie together reading and video game play.

IWAOKA, HISAE. *SATURN APARTMENTS*. SAN FRANCISCO: VIZ MEDIA

This series is definitely better suited for older tweens. It has a more science fiction–type storyline, with people no longer able to inhabit Earth. A book talk would be helpful to encourage tweens to check it out.

SONISHI, KENJI. *LEAVE IT TO PET!* SAN FRANCISCO: VIZ MEDIA

The main character is a nine-year-old boy, and the recycling theme is gender neutral. While tending to be a bit more popular with girls, this series is read by both genders.

YAGINUMA, KOU. *TWIN SPICA*. NEW YORK: VERTICAL

This series follows high school students preparing to become astronauts. The main character is female, but the other supporting characters are male. It is an interesting premise and one that could appeal to a variety of tweens.

YOYO. *VERMONIA*. NEW YORK: ROSEN

A group of four teens who have fantastical adventures in a different world will appeal to many different groups of tweens. It is vaguely reminiscent of *Power Rangers*, but in this case the teens have different powers in different worlds.

Yu-Gi-Oh! SAN FRANCISCO: VIZ MEDIA

There are so many story arcs, or subseries, within the *Yu-Gi-Oh!* universe. Most variations have different authors, but they continue to be perennial favorites with tweens, especially those who play the card game.

Mystery

When thinking about tween mysteries, most adults' brains will go to some of the classic series of their youth or that of their parents. *Encyclopedia Brown, Nancy Drew*, and *Hardy Boys* still have a place in the tween canon of mysteries (and in fact usually are the backbone of the collection). Of course, one could argue that the *Boxcar Children* books also belong in the tween section, but, depending on how youth books in general are grouped, librarians may include this series with books for slightly younger children. There are always good standalone tween mystery books, but trying to find more contemporary strictly mystery titles is a bit more difficult. Frequently the mystery books for tweens are also action/adventure or part of a more fantasy or science fiction like book instead. These books in this section reflect a more traditional and narrow view of the mystery genre.

BALLIETT, BLUE. *HYDE PARK*. NEW YORK: SCHOLASTIC PRESS

While this series has been out for a while, there is something intriguing about the puzzles that appear throughout the stories. The main characters are tweens themselves, so there is a lot that tween readers can identify with.

BOSCH, PSEUDONYMOUS. *SECRET*. NEW YORK: LITTLE, BROWN BOOKS
FOR YOUNG READERS

These books feature mysterious goings on with tween protagonists. However, the snarky narrator makes this series a possibility for some reluctant readers or those tweens who are required to read a mystery book for a school assignment but declare they do not like mysteries.

DIXON, FRANKLIN W. *HARDY BOYS*

The *Hardy Boys* and *Nancy Drew* series seem inextricably linked, and not just because of the 1970s television shows. Just about anything said for one series can be said about the other. The *Hardy Boys* now have updated stories and adventures for tweens, although many libraries probably still have the classic and original books, which can be moved to the tween section. Nostalgia for fathers and grandfathers will be strong, and this can lead them to want their tween sons and grandsons to love the *Hardy Boys* books as well.

FULLER, KATHLEEN. *MYSTERIES OF MIDDLEFIELD.* NASHVILLE: THOMAS NELSON

With just three books in this series, it is both a mystery and a Christian fiction story. Depending on the community, it may fit better in a Christian or inspirational fiction section. This series is a good reminder that there can be books that fit in more than one section, so you will need to consider what genre will get the books read more often. It is also a good time to remind librarians that there may be local authors either self-publishing or working with small local presses that provide good-quality books for tweens but will not appear in national review journals.

GRISHAM, JOHN. *THEODORE BOONE.* NEW YORK: DUTTON BOOKS FOR YOUNG READERS

More than once rabid adult John Grisham fans have arrived in their local library with a question about "this new John Grisham series that they heard/read about and why aren't they with the other John Grisham books on the shelf?" Of course, that requires explaining that this series is shelved with the other tween mysteries. *Theodore Boone* is an enjoyable series and worth mentioning to both adults and tweens. However, since Grisham is a well-known adult author, that may make adults more likely to pick up the books for their tweens.

KEENE, CAROLYN. *NANCY DREW*

Pay attention to the newest repackaging and updating of this perennial favorite female detective. As we've mentioned before, this series will have huge nostalgia appeal for parents and grandparents. However, keep in mind that there are lots of reimagined stories about Nancy Drew for many different ages, including younger readers. However, the main audience for *Nancy Drew* is tweens.

LANE, ANDREW. *SHERLOCK HOLMES: THE LEGEND BEGINS.* NEW YORK: FARRAR, STRAUS, GIROUX

With the popularity of Benedict Cumberbatch's portrayal of Sherlock Holmes, there seems to be a resurgence of interest in this classic character. This series explores what Sherlock was like as a teenager, and there is a lot of appeal for tweens with that idea. It is also a great way to eventually get precocious older tweens interested in reading the original Sir Arthur Conan Doyle books.

SNICKET, LEMONY. *ALL THE WRONG QUESTIONS.* NEW YORK: LITTLE, BROWN BOOKS FOR YOUNG READERS

This series has much in common stylistically with Snicket's *A Series of Unfortunate Events*. Tweens will continue to enjoy the never-ending disasters that befall the main character, and no matter how bad things are in the readers' lives, they are surely better than the events in the life of young Lemony.

SOBOL, DONALD J. *ENCYCLOPEDIA BROWN*

Short episodic mysteries can be good for reluctant readers. Sometimes the stories feel a bit dated, but these are still worthwhile books to have around, especially for parents and grandparents to wax nostalgic about and borrow for the tweens in their lives.

WEINER, ELLIS. *TEMPLETON TWINS.* SAN FRANCISCO: CHRONICLE BOOKS

Hopefully there will be more books published in this series, but the tween protagonists have a snarky narrator to "help" them through their story. It is definitely something to recommend to tweens who like any of Lemony Snicket's or Pseudonymous Bosch's books.

Nonfiction

Obviously tweens are going to need quality nonfiction books for school projects. However, this list focuses on groups of books that they will want to read for pleasure. Sometimes nonfiction books can be great options for reluctant readers who believe that reading is only for books with narratives, not facts and directions. Reading is reading, and educational research indicates that reading nonfiction is beneficial for tweens in the long run. Then, of course, there are lots of great nonfiction series to choose from. However, there are several series included here that could and should be listed under fiction. They are in this section because the ability to pair fiction and nonfiction books about the same topic is a great way to encourage tweens to read more nonfiction. As for where to put tween nonfiction, that can be a challenge, and one that will be determined by the parameters of the library. Is the youth nonfiction collection meant for a specific range of ages? Is all nonfiction, regardless of reading level, mixed together? Is it possible to simply use a sticker or some type of flag to indicate which books are good for tweens and leave them where they are? There is no perfect way to do things. This section should remind librarians that tweens may want to read nonfiction for pleasure, and there are many interesting things to recommend to them.

DK Eyewitness Books. New York: DK Publishing

It is possible to make the argument that these books are great for getting information for school projects on scientific and historical topics. However, the counterargument is that, with the many quality images filling up the pages and superb organization, these books can be read a little bit at a time for fun. For tweens interested in a particular topic, or ones who like books with lots of pictures, these books are great. Even better, they are updated every few years, so the information is current and correct. What's not to like?

Guinness World Records. New York: Guinness World Records

Whether it's the annual volume or specialized thematic volumes, the Guinness World Record books are perennially popular with tweens. There are so many things to read, consider, and even persuade parents to let them try. And while many tweens don't view this as reading, it most certainly is!

Ologies. Somerville: Candlewick Press

Though fabulous and fantastic, the many pieces, parts, and pockets that come with these books may be a no-go for some libraries. There are things to be lost after being borrowed, but if these books are in the library, tweens will love them. This series is sometimes placed in folklore sections of libraries. While it is most definitely a fictional series, tweens enjoy its organization, and it can sometimes prompt interest in more truly nonfiction books on the same topics.

Ripley's Believe It or Not. New York: Scholastic

Sometimes this can be shelved in the adult nonfiction section, but tweens have an affinity for the strange information contained within the book. It is like the *Guinness Book of World Records* and even various almanacs; there is so much information to read and absorb! And for many tweens, particularly boys, the stranger the information, the better!

Scholastic Almanac for Kids. New York: Scholastic

Whether you purchase this specific almanac or something similar, there will be some tweens who just love facts. Certainly there are tons of facts all over the Internet, but this is one of those occasions when a wide variety of facts located in one easy-to-hold place may be advantageous. The one thing to keep in mind is how many "old" almanacs are on the library's shelves, as it is not the best idea to have tweens memorizing and repeating outdated information.

SCHWARTZ, ALVIN. *SCARY STORIES.* NEW YORK: HARPERCOLLINS

The perennial favorites of campouts and sleepovers, these books contain creepy stories that have stood the test of time. Regardless of whether they are shelved in fiction or folklore, tweens love these stories. Use these books to introduce tweens to other volumes of folklore, urban legends, and creepy stories.

SILVERSTEIN, SHEL

Shel Silverstein's poetry has been around since the 1970s, but several books have been published posthumously. Poetry also counts as reading, despite what many tweens may think. And while there are lots of great poets writing for children and tweens, this classic author is listed for the benefit of parents and grandparents with fond memories of *Where the Sidewalk Ends* and *A Light in the Attic.* Silverstein's work can be used as a gateway to introduce tweens to other poets (and it does not have to be solely during Poetry Month).

TARSHIS, LAUREN. *I SURVIVED.* NEW YORK: SCHOLASTIC

These are not nonfiction titles, but they can easily be paired with nonfiction to provide factual support for the events thus depicted. Many tweens find these books at the ubiquitous school book fairs. Being prepared with information about these same events is worthwhile for libraries.

THE VISUAL DICTIONARY. NEW YORK: DK PUBLISHING

"Visual Dictionary" is the subtitle for many DK titles. However, these are not actual dictionaries, but rather LEGO or *Star Wars* books. Every library should have a copy of all of these books so tweens can pore over the information contained within. Also keep an eye open for DK titles that have "Complete Encyclopedia" in the subtitle.

YOU WOULDN'T WANT TO.... NEW YORK: FRANKLIN WATTS

Focusing on different periods in history, this series is snarky, revolting, and really informative. There is a new series, *You Wouldn't Want to Live Without ...* that focuses on aspects of everyday life and what would happen if these elements were no longer around. However, the original historical books bring parts of history to life in a visceral way for tweens to enjoy and devour.

Science Fiction

It can be argued that sometimes the lines between science fiction and fantasy are blurred or that authors who write in one genre tend to write in another. It can also be said that some of the books in other genres, like action, mystery, or even the supernatural, may contain some elements of science fiction. However, the following list includes some contemporary and classic science fiction titles. Of course, the "classic" science fiction could also be shelved among the other classics, if that makes sense in a particular library. Just be aware that there will be passionate tweens (and probably adults) wanting to discuss with librarians why a book is placed in science fiction instead of some other place. If that is the case, congratulations! This means there are patrons who feel comfortable enough to come and talk to the librarian about what is happening with "their" books.

FARMER, NANCY. *THE EAR, THE EYE, AND THE ARM*

Having been published a while ago, this book is probably already in many libraries. This science fiction title could potentially count as a mystery title, since the plot centers around a kidnapping. However, it is much more of a science fiction book.

FARMER, NANCY. *THE HOUSE OF THE SCORPION.* NEW YORK: ATHENEUM BOOKS

Nancy Farmer writes both fantasy and science fiction. This Newbery Honor book is a thought-provoking read that can interest a lot of tweens who are curious about the "what ifs" of future society.

HADDIX, MARGARET PETERSON. *MISSING.* NEW YORK: SIMON & SCHUSTER BOOKS FOR YOUNG READERS

Time travel is the focus of this series, and it has plenty of boy appeal. However, tweens of either gender will enjoy it. Books by Margaret Haddix are a solid choice to have within the science fiction genre.

HADDIX, MARGARET PETERSON. *SHADOW CHILDREN.* NEW YORK: SIMON & SCHUSTER BOOKS FOR YOUNG READERS

A futuristic society dominates this series. Again, it has lots of boy appeal, but the action will interest both genders. This is another great science fiction series to have in the tween collection that most assuredly will be found somewhere else in the library.

L'ENGLE, MADELINE. *TIME QUINTET*

This series may also be referred to as the "Murray Family Time Quintet," but this may be a shorthand way of collecting the books that include the characters first introduced in *A Wrinkle in Time.* While the first book was a Newbery winner and is generally considered a classic, the remaining books in the series have also remained popular over time. These books, in order, are *A Wrinkle in Time, A Wind in the Door, A Swiftly Tilting Planet, Many Waters,* and *An Acceptable Time.*

LOWRY, LOIS. *GIVER QUARTET*

Beginning with the Newbery Award–winning book *The Giver*, this series was one of the early dystopian fiction offerings for tweens and young adults before the *Hunger Games* and *Divergent* series became wildly popular. It is also great to pair *The Giver* book and movie together.

PATTERSON, JAMES. *DANIEL X.* NEW YORK: LITTLE, BROWN

This series could be quite legitimately placed in the action genre instead of science fiction. James Patterson has books for tweens that cross many different genres. He writes this series with his frequent tween book collaborator, Chris Grabenstein.

PATTERSON, JAMES. *HOUSE OF ROBOTS.* NEW YORK: LITTLE, BROWN

You may want to put this series in with humorous stories instead of science fiction, and it will most likely appeal to younger tweens. As always, it is imperative to consider how to define the different genres. Do books that contain definite scientific elements like robots, time travel, futuristic settings, or even aliens belong solely in science fiction, or does the entire story need to be evaluated to see whether the book or series would fit into the tween collection best in another location?

SCARROW, ALEX. *TIMERIDERS.* NEW YORK: WALKER & COMPANY

Time travel is always an interesting topic for tweens to read about. The premise of this series is that teens are able to travel through time to keep historical events happening as they should. These books will most likely appeal to older tweens.

STAR WARS

These will be existing books directed at the tween audience that expand upon the *Star Wars* canon. There are always new books coming out. These books, while originally based on the movie franchise, have grown to include expanded stories and characters, giving a legitimate reason why they should be included in science fiction instead of the genre that focuses on media tie-ins.

Seen on TV

This section is different from others because there are no suggested books, as this part of the collection is the most ephemeral. Something may be popular only for a few months or, at best, a few years. This is the area that will need to be weeded the most often, because things will become passé quickly. However, if this is a section that the library decides to include in the tween collection, and it is a popular collection of books, call it "Seen on TV" or "New at the Movies," or something similar. This area is for the books that have a BISAC heading of "Juvenile Fiction, Media

Tie-In." If tweens recognize the library as a place that tries (and sometimes even succeeds) to carry what is currently popular, the institution will garner much "street cred."

Regarding how to begin or expand this genre, book vendors produce either paper or online catalogs of items that will be available soon. More than likely media tie-in books will be aimed at younger tweens. But keep in mind that if an "old" or even more recent book or book series becomes a big-budget movie or popular television show, the library will need to make sure the tweens know that the books came first. Also, let the tweens tell what movies they cannot wait to see or the television shows they binge watch on DVR or whatever streaming services they use. Use that information to further develop and modify this genre within the collection.

Supernatural/Horror

Some libraries, if they have a lot of ghost stories that aren't necessarily super scary, will break out supernatural from horror. Or perhaps there are tweens who like the idea of having a horror section where scary books are located. This will include stories of ghosts, werewolves, vampires, and basically "things that go bump in the night." Given the long-term popularity of books like *Twilight* and television shows like *Supernatural*, *Vampire Diaries*, and *iZombie*, tweens are still very much interested in the supernatural. However, if this subject is not of huge interest in the community, many of these books can be categorized as fantasy and shelved there. This genre also can end up including books that would fit well in action or adventure. Listen to the tweens. They will make it clear if this narrow genre is truly necessary within their collection.

DANESHVARI, GITTY. *SCHOOL OF FEAR.* NEW YORK: LITTLE,
   BROWN BOOKS FOR YOUNG READERS

This trilogy is listed in the supernatural genre because it serves as a reminder to keep an open mind about classifying books. While this series does not have traditional supernatural elements, as many other series do, it deals with fears and other elements that are frequently associated with books about the supernatural.

DELANEY, JOSEPH. *LAST APPRENTICE.* NEW YORK:
   GREENWILLOW BOOKS

This book series could arguably end up in the young adult book collection; it is definitely aimed at older tweens. Knowing the community will indicate where this series best belongs. With that said, it could also fit in the adventure or fantasy genres. The books follow Thomas Ward as he grows and develops over time while learning to be a Spook—one who fights evil supernatural forces.

DONBAVAND, TOMMY. *SCREAM STREET*. SOMERVILLE:
 CANDLEWICK PRESS

At the outset this series could appear similar to the *Goosebumps* books given the different supernatural elements in each volume. However, it does have a humorous element as well. These books will appeal to younger tweens.

HAHN, MARY DOWNING

Mary Downing Hahn has been writing ghost stories and tales of the supernatural for a long time, and most libraries are sure to have copies of many of her books. These are great books to anchor the supernatural or horror genres.

HOROWITZ, ANTHONY

While Horowitz is known as the author of the tween adventure series *Alex Rider*, he has also written several books of short horror stories. These would be good to give tweens who have already read Alvin Schwartz's *Scary Stories* series.

JOBLING, CURTIS. *WEREWORLD*. NEW YORK: VIKING BOOKS
 FOR YOUNG READERS.

This is definitely a series that fits well in the fantasy genre, but since the werewolves are considered supernatural creatures, the series can belong in more than one area. It could also arguably be an action or adventure series.

NIGHT, P.J. *YOU'RE INVITED TO A CREEPOVER*. NEW YORK:
 SIMON SPOTLIGHT

This series is written in the tradition of spooky stories, with different supernatural and scary elements appearing in the different books. It is not too scary, but it is not babyish by any means.

SAGE, ANGIE. *ARAMINTA SPOOKIE*. NEW YORK:
 KATHERINE TEGEN BOOKS

In addition to the original series, there is *Araminta Spookie Adventures*, which is a second series featuring the same main character. This series could belong in the humorous books, but the characters themselves all fit within the supernatural genre.

STINE, R.L. *GOOSEBUMPS*. NEW YORK: SCHOLASTIC

Any library is sure to have *Goosebumps* books somewhere in its collection. This has to be one of the quintessential tween series, and there are many books and several subseries to choose from. The original *Goosebumps* books are now *Goosebumps Classics*, and there are also *Goosebumps Horrorland* and *Goosebumps Most Wanted*.

WINKLER, HENRY. *GHOST BUDDY.* NEW YORK: SCHOLASTIC

While this series could also be placed in the collection of humorous books, the relationship between Billy Broccoli and Hoover Porterhouse will appeal to younger tweens in particular.

The Takeaway

All sorts of books are necessary in the tween collection. Suggestions have been provided in the preceding pages, but there are far more titles to choose from than have been listed here. There are different genres and subgenres, and often books can belong in more than one place.

- Action/adventure books are just that. There is a lot of movement and activity. These are high-energy stories.
- Fantasy is a huge genre. There can be light fantasy and traditional fantasy books; both categories have a place in the library.
- Classics can be books that have stood the test of time, or they can be award winners. Sometimes they are both.
- General fiction covers a wide range of topics, including sports, animals, historical fiction, and contemporary narratives.
- Chick lit is going to be a girls-only group of books.
- Graphic novels can cover topics from light to serious and tell stories with both images and words.
- Humorous books can be the mainstay of a tween collection.
- Manga are like graphic novels, but paying attention to the suggested age ranges is wise.
- Mystery books have a small but devoted following, and they are necessary elements of the tween collection.
- Nonfiction books, whether they are separate from the rest of the tween collection or not, are important to remind tweens that they can read more than fictional narratives.
- Science fiction frequently overlaps with action/adventure books.
- "Seen on TV" is a great place for media tie-in books.
- Supernatural/horror is a popular genre right now, since there are a lot of television shows of the same genre.

14

Books for the Reluctant Reader

Let's look at the books themselves first. Books for tweens generally do not contain a lot of pictures. Current early chapter books, intended for slightly younger children, still will have an illustration or two in every chapter, and the font size is larger. Tween books, by contrast, feature more text on each page. It could be argued that the book collections become more introspective, and maybe even feminine in focus, at the tween level as opposed to early chapter books. The stories are more journeys of the mind and self-discovery than they are books of action and suspense. This is not to say that there are no adventurous stories—there are certainly some of those types of books in the tween section—but book reports and other school restraints tend to push the reading toward more "girly books," as some tweens have been wont to say.

By the tween stage, school has become much more complicated, frequently with a lot more homework as well. Once upon a time homework was reading a book you liked for 15 minutes each night, or something like that. Now there are reports, presentations, and readings from textbooks that must be completed between the Scouting, church, artistic, and sports activities that fill much of tweens' afterschool time. There is more pressure in school in general. There is testing and preparing for high school, and reading can be an extension of school work. It is no longer fun. In this environment, learning disabilities or challenges can rise to the surface as school becomes more complicated.

Librarians know from their own experiences that children who see the people in their family reading are more likely to be readers themselves. Are tweens seeing the adults in their lives reading? When the adults have to run around to take tweens to activities and participate in different things related to work and after work, there is not much time for them to be reading. As much as tweens are trying to separate from their parents, they still look to them for cues for what they should be doing. If they do not see the adults in their lives reading, they will not do so, either.

Peer pressure—it is the "elephant in the room." It can be both a good and a bad thing for tweens. Tweens with friends who do not read probably will not read themselves. What a peer group is doing will influence a tween's choices, for better or for worse. Particularly for boys, it has become a cultural norm that by the time they become tweens they are playing sports and video games, not doing things like reading.

Girls can read, but among boys it is not as readily acceptable. However, librarians know there are books that they have seen practically every tween boy reading. Unfortunately, that is the exception to the rule.

Even knowing that many tweens seem to at some point decide for any number of reasons mentioned earlier that they are not going to read anymore, there are some ways to get those tweens to find a book, read it, and like it. This is not to say that only reluctant readers are interested in funny books and graphic novels. In fact, these types of books are quite popular with most tweens. However, when facing tweens who, for whatever reason, need a book to read but perhaps do not want a book to read, these two genres are great.

Whether the library groups books by genres, puts genre stickers on books, or does nothing specifically except keep an eye on the subject heading assigned by book ordering companies, knowing what the library has in terms of graphic novels or humorous stories is beneficial. There is also a less talked-about subgenre that can sometimes be called "media tie-in," which refers to books related to contemporary movies or television shows. These three types of books can appeal to reluctant readers, and they were mentioned earlier in chapter 13.

Media tie-in books can work well for the reluctant reader who has already seen the movie or television show that the book is about. Coming to the book with previous information about characters and plot can help, particularly when dealing with learning disabilities, challenges with comprehension, or problems involving any of the actual strategies of reading. The previous understanding of the characters is helpful even and especially when the books are taking aspects of the television show, movie, or even video game and expanding upon the story previously told (*Star Wars* is a good example of this concept; there are a large number of novels for a variety of age groups that expand the stories originally told in the movies). However, in general, it is impossible to provide a list of good media tie-in books. What is interesting and popular on television and in the movies changes too quickly. Suffice it to say that being aware of and having materials that complement what is currently popular will help reluctant readers. For librarians, this is where knowledge of pop culture is invaluable.

Keep in mind that all tweens, not just reluctant readers, are extremely conscious of how they appear to their age group. Also, in this age of social media, when a picture or video can be posted instantaneously and shared with hundreds of followers, the need to "save face" is hugely important. If a reluctant reader is reading below grade level, then walking around with a "baby book" is not going to be acceptable. Humorous books and particularly graphic novels really work well in the "appearances are everything" arena. While there are some humorous books that are quite long and text heavy, quite a few are not. These types of books are acceptable to almost all tweens.

The *Diary of a Wimpy Kid* series is a wonderful choice for reluctant readers for several reasons, and it illustrates some traits that good reluctant reader books have in common. The books are a mix of illustrations and text; they are not so text heavy that they become difficult to read, but they are not so full of pictures as to seem babyish. It is such a popular series that it gave rise to several movies, which brings a certain cool factor to the books. Even the books that have not yet been turned into movies are perfectly okay to read. Within most of the books there is some amount of bodily humor or simply jokes that are funny mostly to tweens. The "cheese touch" is one of the most famous examples of this from the book series, but each book has a certain "stupid joke" component to it.

Graphic novels are another wonderful type of book to recommend to reluctant readers. Lots of librarians have talked for years about the benefits of graphic novels for all readers, particularly those who might be struggling. In this case, graphic novels benefit in their "cool factor" from the idea that many adults, mostly outside the library profession, believing that reading graphic novels (or comic books) is not truly *reading*. The cachet and coolness of a graphic novel is immediately raised for tweens when someone in their life believes that this does not count as reading or is not appropriate. In terms of understanding, the image-heavy graphic novel can provide the reader with many important clues and cues about the story; thus a more complex story can be told. There is a growing body of graphic novels that are also media tie-ins to video games and movies. As stated earlier, if readers have some previous understanding of the characters due to having watched the movie or played the game, this will make the graphic novels easier to understand. And sometimes the slim profile of a graphic novel seems less daunting than a chunky book. However, if it is a thin book, it had best have a mature-looking cover so it isn't perceived as a "baby book."

The most important thing for librarians to remember about reluctant readers is their ability to influence them. A book will work for a reluctant reader in a particular community that does not work for another reader somewhere else if the librarian making the recommendation likes the book and sells it well. His or her ability to sell the book to a tween because they like it, or because it has a particular element that they know will work for this specific tween, is priceless. Knowing the community will indicate the types of books that work best for reluctant readers. However, having a good supply of these types of books is always going to be worthwhile.

The following is a list of books that, for a variety of reasons, may be good to recommend to reluctant reader tweens.

Graphic Novels

There are several publishers that produce much-loved graphic novels. Even before getting to the selection of graphic novels themselves, it is worth drawing attention to some publishers that consistently provide good materials for tween collections. Listing these publishers in alphabetical order will not appear to give one publisher more importance than another. Also, there are many great publishers of graphic novels for tweens; the ones listed below are simply those whose work we have found useful over time. Some publishers to watch may produce books that are either a little too young or a little too old for tweens, but having a general idea of what is happening within the graphic novel genre as a whole helps librarians determine what is good for the tween collection.

1. Abdo Spotlight—This is a specific imprint within the larger Abdo Publishing Company. While not exclusively publishing graphic novels, it does have quite a catalog of graphic novels about superheroes and *Star Wars*. Later on certain series will be noted specifically, but keep an eye on what is being offered.

2. Archie Comics—Beyond the "old school" Archie comics, there are a couple of other titles this company publishes that are worth paying attention to for tweens.

3. Boom! Studios—This company publishes more graphic novels that are media tie-ins to television, movies, and web comics. While some offerings may be inappropriate for tweens, knowing that this is a place to check for media tie-in materials is important.

4. First Second—This publisher has released most of Gene Luen Yang's graphic novels. Its publications may not necessarily be the first books reluctant readers pick up. However, these are great titles to recommend to parents and teachers.

5. Graphix—This is part of the Scholastic family. It produces several collections that will be part of most libraries' tween graphic novel collection.

6. Papercutz—This is another publisher of many great tween graphic novels, several of which will be highlighted later.

7. Stone Arch—This company's products are not exclusively graphic novels, but a component of its collection includes some graphic novels about superheroes and other characters of interest to tweens.

8. Top Shelf Productions—This publisher tends to produce materials for an older audience, but it also publishes *Owly*, which may be popular with some of the younger tweens.

Batman

There are a variety of graphic novel series that feature Batman. More recently, there is *All-New Batman: The Brave and the Bold* as well as *Batman Strikes!* Since some of Batman's storylines can be very dark, make sure that the Batman graphic novels included in the tween collection match the maturity level of the rest of the collection. Be aware that some tweens will eagerly read *Batman* titles intended for much more mature readers.

BLACKMAN, HADEN. *STAR WARS: DARTH VADER AND THE LOST COMMAND.* EDINA: SPOTLIGHT

This series takes place within a specific period of time in the *Star Wars* chronology. These books are great for the non-readers who know tons of facts about the *Star Wars* movies and/or video games.

CAPTAIN AMERICA. EDINA: SPOTLIGHT

There are a couple of smaller story arcs for Captain America that Spotlight has published. Captain America is popular with tweens both on his own and as part of the Avengers.

DAVIS, JIM. *GARFIELD*

There are both the *Garfield Classics* and *The Garfield Show.* The classics are compilations of the newspaper comic strip, whereas *The Garfield Show* looks more like contemporary graphic novels. Even though Garfield has been around for a long time, he continues to attract tweens and repeated readings.

ENGLEHART, STEVE. *JURASSIC PARK.* EDINA: SPOTLIGHT

While *Jurassic Park* has been a perennially popular series of films, be aware that for some tweens, these books may not be appropriate. However, this series can be a good recommendation for tweens who have already watched the movies.

FLYNN, IAN. *MEGA MAN.* MAMARONECK: ARCHIE COMICS

Getting bound collections of comics originally published in traditional paper comic form is advantageous for most libraries due to their ability to be circulated long term. This particular series is often popular with tweens who are also fans of *Sonic the Hedgehog.*

GUARDIANS OF THE GALAXY. EDINA: SPOTLIGHT

Written by a variety of authors, these books have become more popular due to the movie release a few years ago.

IRON MAN. EDINA: SPOTLIGHT

There are several story arcs, usually four bound volumes each, that Spotlight has published. With Robert Downey Jr. as the a successful and popular Tony Stark, Iron Man continues to be a popular Marvel superhero for tweens.

KIBUISHI, KAZU. *AMULET.* NEW YORK: GRAPHIX

This may be more of a stretch for reluctant readers, as it is not quite as bright and eye-catching as some of the other graphic novels. However, the story could serve as a way of bringing reluctant or struggling readers to adventure and fantasy stories that are primarily text.

MARTIN, ANN M. *THE BABY-SITTERS CLUB GRAPHIX.*
   NEW YORK: GRAPHIX

The first several books of Martin's popular tween series have now been released as graphic novels. In this form, they have become quite popular with tween girls where the paperback books have long since been discarded from many years of wear and tear.

MARVEL ADVENTURES. NEW YORK: MARVEL COMICS GROUP

This overarching series encompasses a variety of books about different Marvel superheroes, including Spider-Man, the Avengers, the Hulk, and Iron Man. These graphic novels are the size of small chapter books, but they are great to recommend to reluctant readers who have enjoyed any or all of the recent Marvel movies.

MILLER, JOHN JACKSON. *STAR WARS: KNIGHT ERRANT.*
   EDINA: SPOTLIGHT

Taking place many years before the time of the popular movies, this is great for tweens who are very much aware of and love *Star Wars*.

PARKER, JEFF. *AVENGERS.* EDINA: SPOTLIGHT

There are lots of Avengers graphic novels. These particular ones from Spotlight, part of Abdo, are appropriate for tweens, and, in combination with the well-received movies, they are an easy sell to tweens.

PARKER, JEFF. *FANTASTIC FOUR.* EDINA: SPOTLIGHT

No library can go wrong with more graphic novels about superheroes. They seem so popular right now.

PEIRCE, LINCOLN. *BIG NATE COMIC COMPILATIONS.* KANSAS CITY, MO:
   ANDREWS MCMELL

Big Nate was an online comic strip long before it became a well-loved series of humorous books. Reluctant readers can enjoy both the comic compilations and the stories told in a more narrative form.

PEYO. *SMURFS.* NEW YORK: PAPERCUTZ

These aren't quite the 1980s cartoon Smurfs that tweens' parents watched. Regardless, the graphic novels are still a fun read for tweens.

RAICHT, MIKE. *HULK.* EDINA: SPOTLIGHT

These graphic novels about the Hulk have been out for quite a while, relatively speaking. However, they continue to be good for tweens who like Hulk and want to read more about him.

SMITH, JEFF. *BONE.* NEW YORK: GRAPHIX

This series has been around for a long time, but tweens continue to love reading these books. They are a perennial recommendation for tween reluctant readers, and they are book fair staples.

SONIC. MAMARONECK: ARCHIE COMIC

There are several subseries within the broader series about the popular video game character Sonic the Hedgehog, including *Sonic Archives, Sonic Universe, Sonic Saga, Sonic the Hedgehog,* and *Sonic Boom.* These will probably appeal to the younger tweens or any tween who enjoys playing the Sonic games.

STAR WARS: INFINITES. EDINA: SPOTLIGHT

These books also work for the *Star Wars* aficionado who does not enjoy or has trouble reading but knows everything about *Star Wars.*

STINE, R.L. *GOOSEBUMPS GRAPHIX.* NEW YORK: GRAPHIX

Several of Stine's *Goosebumps* books have been turned into graphic novels, similar to how some of the *Baby-Sitters Club* books have now become graphic novels.

THOR. EDINA: SPOTLIGHT

There are stories just about Thor as well as those that have him collaborating with Iron Man. Even though Thor did not have a prominent role in the most recent Avengers movie, he is still a popular superhero.

TRANSFORMERS

There have been some graphic novels about the Transformers published by both IDW Publishing and Spotlight, all of which are appropriate for tweens. It has been a while since the movies came out, but you can still do a book and movie combination push for reluctant readers. Also, tweens' parents may remember the animated show from the 1980s.

WOLVERINE. EDINA: SPOTLIGHT

Potentially the most famous of the X-Men, Wolverine has his own set of graphic novels for tweens. There are also movies to pair with the books.

X-MEN: FIRST CLASS. EDINA: SPOTLIGHT

While the X-Men movies may not be as popular with tweens as the Marvel Avenger movies, it is still worthwhile to pair the book and movie for X-Men titles. Do not discount the possibilities of tweens' parents wanting to tell their children about how much they loved the movies or comics growing up.

Humorous

Fortunately, there are many publishers that produce humorous books for tweens. Many of these books have a primary audience of tween boys. Not all reluctant readers are boys, but girls tend to read books that might be intended for boys, whereas the reverse is usually not true. Often these books can seem irreverent and potentially offensive to adults who might not appreciate the type of humor that is common in these books. However, having plenty of these offerings available for anyone who needs a "funny book" will stand a librarian and the library in good stead.

ANGLEBERGER, TOM. *FAKE MUSTACHE: OR, HOW JODIE O'RODEO AND HER WONDER HORSE (AND SOME NERDY KID) SAVED THE PRESIDENTIAL ELECTION FROM A MAD GENIUS.* NEW YORK: AMULET BOOKS

The ridiculously long subtitle just adds to the joy of the book. The author is a solid tween writer. Even though this did not gain as much attention as the *Origami Yoda* series, it is still a silly read for tweens.

ANGLEBERGER, TOM. *HORTON HALFPOTT: OR THE FIENDISH MYSTERY OF SMUGWICK MANOR; OR, THE LOOSENING OF M'LADY LUGGERTUCK'S CORSET.* NEW YORK: ABRAMS

This is also a long subtitle of silliness. It definitely appeals to tweens' interest in bodily humor and general absurdity.

ANGLEBERGER, TOM. *ORIGAMI YODA.* NEW YORK: AMULET BOOKS

This series of books is funny regardless of whether a tween is a *Star Wars* fan. The interactions between friends and the crises of middle schoolers are presented in an easily understandable way. This series is a good mix of images and text, making it a great book for reluctant readers.

ANGLEBERGER, TOM. *QWIKPICK PAPERS.* NEW YORK: AMULET BOOKS

This series is intended for slightly younger tweens. However, it still has the same bodily humor and crazy adventures that make it a solid choice for reluctant readers.

BONIFACE, WILLIAM. *EXTRAORDINARY ADVENTURES OF ORDINARY BOY.* NEW YORK: HARPERCOLLINS

Among the many superhero books available, this is about one ordinary boy in a community of superheroes. Tweens will appreciate not only the humor throughout the book but also the twist in the plot, so that the ordinary person is in the minority.

BROWN, JEFFREY. *STAR WARS: JEDI ACADEMY.* NEW YORK: SCHOLASTIC

These books about Roan, while connected with *Star Wars*, have nothing to do with the official canon of stories. They are for young tweens, and a love of *Star Wars* is not required to enjoy the books.

BUCKLEY, MICHAEL. *NERDS.* NEW YORK: AMULET BOOKS

Losers becoming superheroes is a great idea that many tweens will appreciate. Thwarting villains is what this group of superheroes must do in each volume of the series.

COLLINS, TIM. *VAMPIRE.* NEW YORK: ALADDIN PAPERBACKS

Collins' stories of Nigel Mullet are hilarious for tweens because he is so earnest and whiny. Tweens will enjoy Nigel's angst over his life situations, and supernatural elements remain popular with this age group.

GREENWALD, TOMMY. *CHARLIE JOE JACKSON.* NEW YORK: ROARING BROOK PRESS

Charlie Joe Jackson is the hero of the reluctant reader. His stories of how to do things (or not) are hilarious and appeal to tweens on so many levels. It is a bit more text heavy than some other popular reluctant reader books, but this is still a solid series to recommend.

HOLT, K.A. *BRAINS FOR LUNCH.* NEW YORK: ROARING BROOK PRESS

Not only does this book have typical tween angst and humor, but it is also told in haiku. It is super short, but the content is definitely for tweens. This could be a perfect book for a reluctant reader, although it could pose a challenge for struggling readers since it is written in haiku.

KINNEY, JEFF. *DIARY OF A WIMPY KID.* NEW YORK: AMULET BOOKS

This series of books has spawned movies and board games, and it ushered in a type of graphic-heavy book that is a slightly older version of a *Captain Underpants*–style story. This series has a lot of street cred, and many kids "who never read" have read at least one of these books. Have lots of copies of these available, if possible.

Section V. Tween Materials

KLOEPFER, JOHN. *ZOMBIE CHASERS*. NEW YORK: HARPERCOLLINS

Sarcastic, gross, and filled with zombies, this is a great combination of elements to attract tween readers. This series is likely to appeal to younger tweens.

MACK, JEFF. *CLUELESS MCGEE*. NEW YORK: PHILOMEL BOOKS

The idea of a bumbling tween detective makes these books similar to the *Timmy Failure* series. However, mysterious happenings and tween humor will make these successful options for tweens.

MARCIONETTE, JAKE. *JUST JAKE*. NEW YORK GROSSET & DUNLAP

Following the common plot of a tween having school-related challenges, Jake is a likeable character whom tweens will identify with. This will appeal most to younger tweens.

NESBO, JO. *DOCTOR PROCTOR'S FART POWDER*. NEW YORK: ALADDIN PAPERBACKS

What is not to like about a series having to do with farts? Bodily humor is always great for reluctant readers (and probably most tweens in general). What also makes this series interesting is that it is set outside the United States.

PASTIS, STEPHAN. *TIMMY FAILURE*. SOMERVILLE: CANDLEWICK PRESS

Timmy's stories could be given to a reluctant reader who must read a mystery for a book report, but they are best kept with other humorous books. Timmy just cannot quite get things together, and his misfortunes will be hilarious for tweens.

PATTERSON, JAMES. *MIDDLE SCHOOL*. NEW YORK: LITTLE, BROWN

This series, written with Chris Tebbetts, is not like the adult mysteries for which Patterson is famous. These books are funny for tweens because they can identify with some of the situations presented. Parents and grandparents of tweens will like and recognize one of their favorite authors, Patterson.

PEIRCE, LINCOLN. *BIG NATE*. NEW YORK: BALZER + BRAY

This series is a combination of text and graphics as opposed to the compilations of the comic strips that were noted previously. Nate Wright seems to have most of the dreaded middle school disasters befall him, some of which, of course, he brings on himself. This is a series similar in content and style to the *Diary of a Wimpy Kid* books.

PILKEY, DAV. *CAPTAIN UNDERPANTS*. NEW YORK: SCHOLASTIC

This is one of the quintessential tween humor series. It predates *Diary of a Wimpy Kid*, and it has long been the province of boys who either did not want to read or needed a little help reading. The illustrations and word play make the stories successful.

RUSSELL, RACHEL RENEE. *DORK DIARIES*. NEW YORK:
ALADDIN PAPERBACKS

These are the diaries of Nikki Maxwell. It is a little bit like *Diary of a Wimpy Kid*, but it is a girl's diary.

SCIESZKA, JON. *SPACEHEADZ*. NEW YORK: SIMON & SCHUSTER BOOKS
FOR YOUNG READERS

This series for younger tweens comes from one of the kings of books for reluctant readers. Jon Scieszka is known for writing funny books that children and tweens want to read, and this series is no different.

SEEGERT, SCOTT. *VORDAK THE INCOMPREHENSIBLE*. NEW YORK:
EGMONT USA

Written from the standpoint of a supervillain, these books appeal to the snarky sense of humor that can be common to tweens. It is an interesting twist on and antidote for the many superhero books that are available for tweens.

SKYE, OBERT. *CREATURE FROM MY CLOSET*. NEW YORK: HENRY HOLT

This series has crazy creatures appearing from the tween main character's closet that are a mixture of two different characters from literature or popular culture. It is a unique premise, and tweens are sure to enjoy the crazy closet monster mash-ups.

STINE, R.L. *ROTTEN SCHOOL*. NEW YORK: HARPERCOLLINS

While best known for the tween series *Goosebumps*, Stine's humorous books are also well worth reading. His humor is perfect for younger tweens.

UREY, GARY. *SUPER SCHNOZ*. PARK RIDGE: ALBERT WHITMAN

This is a unique premise in which a physical abnormality makes a tween a superhero. It will appeal to tweens for many different reasons.

The Takeaway

Reluctant readers may be both tweens who have reading difficulties and tweens who cannot find the right book to engage them. Graphic novels and humorous books are good options that will help tweens find something quick and light to grab their attention. Really understanding all the different materials that are out there is helpful when trying to find a tween something to read.

Section V. Tween Materials

A good book for reluctant readers will:

- have a good balance of illustrations and text;
- often include bodily humor;
- generally focus on the trials of everyday life;
- often include characters from movies or television; and
- be anything a librarian can convincingly sell to a tween.

15

Periodicals for Tweens

Periodicals (or magazines, if you prefer) unfortunately are not as popular as they used to be. While at some libraries they continue to be quite successful, at others they have all but disappeared. There is not a whole lot written for librarians to suggest good magazines. Sometimes there will be a conversation in an electronic discussion group, but it is not the same. However, if it turns out that the library's tweens are interested in magazines, or they would like to try some tween-specific magazines, there are a few suggestions. Whether the library should have magazines and which ones to get would be a great thing to discuss with the tween advisory board or simply tweens who are seen frequently in the library.

The other topic of discussion within this chapter is what we call "periodical comics." Unfortunately, there appears to be even less information available in professional literature and other discussions about choosing periodical comics for tweens. Therefore a majority of the chapter will be devoted to this subject. Some communities may see more tweens reading periodical comics than magazines. Therefore, considering this as a possibility for the tween section, or at least as something to discuss with the tween advisory board, may be worthwhile. Periodical comics would perhaps be what many people think of when they hear the term "comics." These are what people buy in comic shops. These episodic stories, often published monthly and generally about superheroes, frequently can be purchased from the same vendors that libraries use for magazines, although it may be necessary to search these vendors specifically for periodical comics. The term "periodical comics" instead of "graphic novels" is preferred because these days people think of graphic novels as including bound periodical comics. Usually there are at least four of the periodical comics all printed together and bound in one volume of a graphic novel. It is possible to get a lot of circulation from periodical comics when tweens want to keep pace with their stories without waiting for the bound volumes to become available.

The ephemeral nature of periodical comics can pose a challenge at times. Either periodical comics go on for years or they last only a short period of time, perhaps even less than a year. More often than not, they last for a year or two at most. When ordering comics through a magazine jobber in particular, libraries can all of a sudden receive a comic they did not order because the one they did order ceased publication. These companies will often substitute another title so the library still gets the same number of issues it paid for. The magazine provider may think that the two periodical comics are comparable titles, but they may not necessarily be age and content equivalent in the librarian's opinion. However, do not let this possibility keep you from ordering periodical comics if it seems like the tweens would enjoy them.

Even though we said earlier that there is not a lot of information about choosing periodical comics to keep in the library, librarians are not without sources of local information about the community's interest in periodical comics. Obviously librarians will ask the tweens in the library about what periodical comics they read or are interested in. There is also another source: the local comic book store. There may be one in the immediate community, or there may be one a short distance away. It is worth visiting and talking to the owner or sales clerk about what they have stocked and who they see buying which periodical comics. These people will be able to give the librarian a good idea of what tweens are reading. There is also the option of buying periodical comics from the local store as opposed to getting them through a larger vendor. It will probably cost more, but it may be worthwhile to support a local business and get the quality advice that a local comic book store can provide.

There are some other ideas to consider when contemplating adding periodical comics to the collection. What graphic novels do you have already? As stated earlier, some graphic novels are several periodical comics bound together in one volume. Would it make sense to get the periodical comic version of some of the graphic novels? Sometimes the answer is yes; other times it is no. It will depend on the tweens in the community. Additionally, in periodical comics, there can be several different storylines going with the same character. What storyline is appropriate for tweens? As discussed in chapter 14, there are some characters whose storylines need to be carefully considered. *Batman* is the best example of this concept because there are Batman storylines that are appropriate for several different age levels. *Teen Titans* is another good example. There are much more childlike, cutesy *Teen Titans* books for children and young tweens, but the *New 52 Teen Titans* storyline and illustrations are definitely for young adult and older readers. Many superheroes span age ranges, and there may be tweens in the community who regularly read periodical comics that have a content level much more in line with the library's young adult material than the tween material. However, as has been said on a number of occasions, it is an individual library's decision.

With all this said, for both magazines and periodical comics, there are some recommendations to offer. Obviously, as with everything else, this is not an exhaustive list.

Magazines

AMERICAN GIRL MAGAZINE

This magazine may or may not belong in the tween section. It needs to be wherever the *American Girl* books are. Some libraries include these books in the tween collection, and other libraries place them with books for slightly younger children.

BOYS' LIFE

This is one of the few tween magazines for boys. It could be read by young adults, but its interest level falls closer to tweens. Unfortunately, because it has "boy" in the title, it may be a tough sell for some tweens even though it is published by the Boy Scouts of America and Boy Scouts are tweens.

DISCOVERY GIRLS

This publication is advertised as a magazine for preteen girls. It is more of an "issues faced as a tween" kind of magazine as opposed to a girl's pop culture magazine.

J-14

Advertised as a tween and teen celebrity magazine, adopting this publication will be more of a community-by-community kind of decision. It is quite popular and well received.

LEGO CLUB MAGAZINE

This is for LEGO-obsessed tweens. Some tweens may get this magazine at home, but it is definitely something that will get used if LEGOs are popular in the community. It is the official magazine of LEGO.

M

This magazine is pitched to a slightly younger audience than *J-14*. Therefore it is right in line with what most libraries would probably consider their tween age range. It is another celebrity magazine.

NATIONAL GEOGRAPHIC KIDS

This magazine runs into the same potential problem as other magazines with "kids" in the title: tweens may feel this publication is too young for them (and in this case, they may be correct). This magazine really is aimed at children younger than tweens. Nevertheless, it is included for consideration. The website says the magazine is meant for children six and up, which definitely makes it more of a children's magazine.

POPSTAR!

This is yet another celebrity magazine. It is probably more similar to *J-14* than to *M*. However, even though the magazines contain the same kind of information, tweens will often read them all.

SPORTS ILLUSTRATED KIDS

Again, the word "kids" in the title could be problematic. However, this is a long-running sports magazine. If it is currently in the library, take a look at who is reading it more often. If the primary readers are tweens, then put it in the tween collection. If they are younger children, then leave it with the other children's magazines.

TIGER BEAT

This is probably the quintessential celebrity magazine for tweens. It also sits on the border of tween and young adult readership. It tends to be associated with middle school or junior high school girls; the librarian must decide where this fits best for the community.

YOUNG RIDER

This magazine is for the tween girl horse enthusiast. It seems that, regardless of whether tween girls are able to ride horses, there is still something about looking at this magazine and dreaming about having and/or riding a horse that is magical.

YUM FOOD AND FUN FOR KIDS

Given that this magazine title includes the word "kids," it runs the risk of being ignored by tweens as too babyish. It definitely has a cutesy, pastel palette and layout, so the decision of whether to keep this publication in the tween collection will depend on what the community's tweens think of it.

Periodical Comics

LOONEY TUNES

This is an example of a long-running comic that is below tween reading level but has great tween appeal. It has the added bonus of some nostalgia for tweens' parents and grandparents.

MS. MARVEL

This title specifically refers to the storyline with Kamala Khan as Ms. Marvel. This is not a very long-running story as of yet, but it has a lot of interest for tweens since Kamala is 16.

SCOOBY-DOO

This is an example of a periodical comic with a reading level that is definitely below that of the rest of the tween material, but it has a lot of tween appeal. Having begun in the 1960s, it has been around for quite a while.

SONIC

This is another long-running comic that has great tween appeal. It is also frequently purchased in the form of graphic novels. Depending on how popular Sonic the Hedgehog is in the community, librarians may decide to order the periodical comic as well as the bound graphic novels. There is both *Sonic the Hedgehog* and *Sonic Universe*.

TEEN TITANS GO!

This is a tween-appropriate storyline that features the same characters as the television cartoon. This publication should not be confused with the young adult *Teen Titans* from the *New 52* series.

The Takeaway

Hopefully this chapter has provided some ideas to talk over with the tweens in your community. Whether or not periodicals are popular at the library, talking with the tweens about whether they want periodicals for their section is important. Remember to consider both traditional magazines and periodical comics. There is a lot to offer in periodical comics, but it is best to understand what they can be like before purchasing them.

In tween periodicals:

- having "kids" in the title can be a deal breaker;
- there are several seemingly identical tween pop culture magazines;
- some periodical comic characters have storylines for a range of maturity levels; and
- periodical comics can have tween appeal but be below average tween reading level.

16

Audiovisual Materials
for Tweens

There is so much audiovisual (AV) material available to tweens these days. YouTube is huge and tweens can access all kinds of content through this venue and many other places. However, in this chapter the only AV materials that will be described are ones that can be circulated by the library to tweens, such as music CDs, DVDs (or Blu-rays), and video games. This does not include titles that can be borrowed through a library media service like Overdrive, hoopla, or the like. In other words, this chapter discusses items that need shelf space in the tween AV area.

The challenge with much of the AV materials is that they can fall in and out of popularity so quickly. It is hard to give recommendations for specific titles unless they are "classics" because of the ephemeral nature of tweens' fascination with a particular artist, movie, or television show. Many of the recommendations will focus on franchises and series. If a character or set of characters has reached franchise level, then it has some staying power and is worth mentioning. In other cases, a type of material may be described, and it will be up to individual libraries to find out what the most contemporary title or titles are that fit the criteria. Finally, it is helpful to mention that the AV title recommendations are on the conservative side. However, there are some marked departures from this more conservative attitude (the reasons for which will be clear). Each library must consider individual AV items and how they relate to the library's collection development policy and community attitudes. Somehow AV materials can engender more visceral and pronounced concerns than those raised by print materials.

Music CDs

With so many opportunities to download music, chances are the library is not going to have a tremendous number of tween CDs. If there are some, the majority will probably be older releases. There just is not much that is actually on CDs anymore. A lot of what is available is "old people" music and not interesting to tweens. However, there is nothing wrong with having older music in the collection if it is still circulating. The following are some examples of items to include.

Kidz Bop

It seems like there have been Kidz Bop CDs forever. Of course, as mentioned in chapter 15, one must be careful about using the word "kid" as it relates to anything connected with tweens. Where libraries put the Kidz Bop music is going to be influenced by the overall community. Kidz Bop releases sanitized versions of popular songs and will probably appeal more to younger tweens. Kidz Bop is a good example of something that is in the tween section more for the benefit of tweens' parents, some of whom may not want to think about the idea that their tween has heard and sings along with the non-sanitized versions of the same songs as heard on the radio or YouTube. Decide what works best for the community. It is definitely possible that Kidz Bop may be included with other children's music instead.

Movie and Television Show Soundtracks

Interestingly enough, this is where there are still physical CDs being produced. If there is a movie coming to the theater that is expected to be purchased for the tween DVD area later, then go ahead and order the soundtrack for the CD collection. If there is a tween-focused television show (which usually means one on the Disney Channel, Nickelodeon, or their attendant auxiliary channels), and it has a soundtrack or "music inspired by" collection, then go ahead and get that for the tween section. Having these types of CDs in the collection demonstrates to tweens that the librarians are keeping an eye on pop culture.

Old-School Music

The term "old-school music" is a bit of a misnomer, but it will be used to describe a few types of CDs. This category can include early albums by pop stars who have long since crossed over to more adult content, or perhaps music from television stars whose shows are now in reruns but still play all the time or soundtracks from those same perpetually rerunning television shows. One might also opt for CDs from older movies that tweens still love to watch but for which the music may not be readily available from tweens' normal sources. As long as the CDs still circulate, hold on to them. Do not necessarily get rid of something just because it's a few years old.

Popular Middle School or High School Age Singers

This is a hard category to describe because it is a "you know it when you see it" sort of thing. These will be artists getting a lot of Top 40 radio air play. The artists themselves will be generally 18 or younger, at least when they break onto the music scene. As they get older, their music may mature and become inappropriate for a tween audience. Right now, One Direction, Justin Bieber, and Taylor Swift are good examples of artists who didn't initially become famous on a tween-focused television show or starring in a tween-focused movie. However, as the artists got older, the lyrics to their songs became more provocative, and there arose a question of whether they should still be in the tween collection. However, initially the music of these artists was quite appropriate for tweens and wildly popular.

Radio Disney Selections

Back in the day, which was not really all that long ago, Radio Disney would release compilations of songs that were popular on the radio station. While this does not happen that often anymore, take a look at or listen to what is on their playlist. If these artists have CDs out, you need to get them. Frequently the mainstays of the radio station are Disney actors who are musicians as well. It is possible to make the argument that probably only young tweens listen to Radio Disney, but remember, it is necessary to market materials to the parents of tweens as well. Frequently, they want to believe that their tweens are far less worldly than they truly are.

DVDs and Blu-rays

Throughout this section the term "DVD" will be used, but the titles could be in the form of either DVDs or Blu-rays. There are still more things for tweens that are produced just in DVD format at this point. Sometimes tweens have "someone's old something." As a result, it is possible that they themselves do not have a Blu-ray player. DVDs are primarily either movies or television shows. The movies can be big box-office blockbusters, direct-to-DVD sequels, or small-budget films. Television shows can be complete seasons or several episodes. There are also cartoons and anime, both of which have great tween appeal and can be either movie length or television episodes. Interestingly enough, over the last few years there has apparently been an increase in parents of tweens wanting to share with their tweens something they watched during their childhood or tween years. Of course, there is no research to back this up, only anecdotal evidence, but since someone is producing these things on DVD, someone else wants to watch them! With that said, similar types of titles are grouped together into broad categories. There was an earlier mention of needing to watch AV ratings carefully, and that will be discussed in more detail as this chapter progresses.

Contemporary Live-Action Movies

Contemporary live-action movies tend to be rated PG, except when they are not. This is a category that really brings to light the need to understand what the community wants and how it views different types of movies. Generally live-action movies will feature superheroes, adventurous tales, book-to-movie adaptations, and basically anything that might appeal to a tween. However, it seems that there are more exceptions to these rules than actual rules. Among other things, movie adaptations of books are a challenge. Sometimes tween contemporary live-action movies can end up including movies that were based on children's picture books but got a PG rating. It is a community-by-community decision, but sometimes these movies take such a departure from the original books that it does not make sense to put them in the children's area with the original books. This choice breaks the general rule of movies being in the same section as their books. However, some of the later *Harry Potter* movies were rated PG-13, but since the *Harry Potter* books were in the tween area, the movies are there as well. Superhero movies, primarily those coming from the Marvel franchise, tend to rated PG-13. The decision to put a copy of these movies in the tween area is not one to be taken lightly. If an overwhelming number of tweens and parents in the community go to see these movies together in the theater, it may make sense to have copies in the tween section. However, it is best to go to tween parents or the tween advisory board to get more information before making a decision.

Disney Franchise

These are going to be the live-action Disney movies, not the animated full-length movies. There have not been as live-action movies lately, but there will probably be older movies of this sort in the tween DVD collection. The *Pirates of the Caribbean* movies are an example of what to include in this category, but be careful, since *Pirates* is actually rated PG-13 (however, it is also something many young children and tweens saw in the theater).

Superhero Movies

Movies from the Marvel franchise have been mentioned before, but DC has also released some superhero movies that are rated PG-13. These are the movies that may legitimately belong somewhere else in the library unless the library is within a "superhero-loving community" where everyone has already seen the movie in the theater (including those younger than 13). The *Transformers* franchise belongs in this category as well; while not strictly superheroes, these are great tween movies.

"Was a Book First" Movies

This category goes beyond *Harry Potter*, as mentioned earlier, to the newer *Chronicles of Narnia, Diary of a Wimpy Kid, Percy Jackson*, and any number of other book-based movies. Sometimes the movies are faithful to the books, and other times the books and movies seem miles apart in storyline. Keep an eye on which of these movies are rated PG or PG-13. Librarians may need to be prepared to explain to parents why there are more mature movies in the tween section.

Contemporary Animated Movies

These are not going to be the traditional Disney animated movies—not that lots of tweens do not watch these movies, but they may not want to admit it. The movies included in this category tend to be the snarkier PG-rated movies from other studios and companies, such as DreamWorks (which released *Kung Fu Panda*) and Universal (*Despicable Me*). These slightly edgier comedic movies are perfect for tweens. The humor level fits them, and they are not "cartoon movies for babies." Some of these animated movies could also be based on books, such the *How to Train Your Dragon* franchise from DreamWorks. Because of the humor that characterizes tween animated movies, there may be movies that were based on picture books that end up in the tween movie area as well.

Parent and Grandparent Nostalgia Movies

This category can cover quite a range of movies, including animated and live action. These are movies that the library probably has had in the collection for a while. In fact, they were probably in the library on VHS at one point, eventually being replaced with a DVD copy. Some titles now are probably available on Blu-ray as well. Keep in mind that parents and other adults are still trying to exert some control over what is happening their tweens' lives. Sharing a favorite movie is a way to both connect and have some control. This list has just a few titles that will get librarians thinking about what similar titles they might already have in their collection; if there are multiple copies, then could one go in the tween section.

THE BLACK CAULDRON

This was Disney's first animated PG movie. It was based on popular tween books of the day, and it caused a sensation at the time of its initial release. However, it is good to remind tweens that there have been many books made into movies over the years. It is not just a recent phenomenon.

A CHRISTMAS STORY

This movie seems to be either adored or reviled by viewers, but somehow it seems that seeing this movie is a rite of passage. With the main character, Ralphie, being a young tween, there is much for tweens to love in this movie. And there are many parents and grandparents who love it too. Think about other holiday movies that might have a place in the tween collection.

ET

There is something timeless about *ET*. This and a handful of other 1980s movies are fun for tweens to watch, if for no other reason than to laugh at the "old technology."

THE LOVE BUG

This and many other classic live-action Disney movies present a bit of a conundrum. They tend to be rated G, but, for the most part, G-rated movies are put in the children's area, and the interest level is not going to be there. Therefore, many of these movies may end up in the tween area because parents and grandparents will find them and want to watch them with their tweens.

Contemporary Live-Action Television

More and more, tweens are streaming episodes of their favorite television shows on some type of device like a television, tablet, computer, or smartphone. Not as many tween shows are having seasons or episodes produced in DVD format. However, there are still channels that cater primarily to tweens. This is not to say that major networks do not produce programming for tweens, but over the past ten to twenty years the majority of tween programming has shifted to specialty channels.

DISNEY CHANNEL

There is the original Disney Channel and there is also Disney XD, which feature many different programs. These channels show new episodes being produced for their original programming as well as older series that have long since ended but live on in reruns.

NICKELODEON

In addition to the original Nickelodeon (or Nick) Channel, there are Nicktoons and TeenNick. These days there rarely are DVDs released for any of their original programming. However, like Disney, some older shows live on in reruns.

Parent Nostalgia Television

Similar to nostalgia movies, there is also nostalgia television, although the television shows are more commonly the province of tweens' parents who were growing up in the 1980s and 1990s. However, there are more grandparent nostalgia television seasons being released on DVD. As the baby boomers' grandchildren get older, there are more television shows they want to share. The challenge with this type of programming is that it does not have the ratings that accompany contemporary television series. Sometimes a librarian must watch a couple of episodes to decide for sure where the series should be located.

THE BRADY BUNCH

Tweens' parents were watching reruns of this program in their childhood. It seems like everyone had seen at least some *Brady Bunch* episodes. This is one show where grandparents will also sit down and watch.

CLARISSA EXPLAINS IT ALL

There are a number of television series from the early days of Nickelodeon that are now available on DVD. Clarissa is a teenager with an annoying younger brother, and the series is still funny today.

LITTLE HOUSE ON THE PRAIRIE

Whether or not these books are in the tween section, the television show is more appropriate for tweens in terms of content. Many parents grew up watching Laura Ingalls and her family living out west.

THE MUPPET SHOW

While only on the air for a few seasons, this series was a cultural phenomenon. Many tweens may not realize that the Muppets were on more than just Sesame Street and a handful of contemporary movies. Even if contemporary tweens do not recognize the then-famous guest stars, many of the sketches in between guest appearances are still funny and appeal to tweens' senses of humor.

Contemporary Cartoons

Even though Saturday morning cartoons are a thing of the past, there are plenty of places where tweens can watch cartoons. Generally cartoons seem to revolve around particular franchises or are owned by specific networks.

DC PROPERTIES

DC Comics has been most successful with various animated incarnations of Batman. Thus far these shows have been rated TV-Y7. They have not been very long-lived series, but they are popular.

DISNEY PROPERTIES

Disney owns several channels and either produces or owns the right to show many different cartoons. The company also has the rights to all of the Marvel cartoons, which tend to be rated TV-Y or TV-Y7. With owning the rights to Marvel, there are quite a few superhero cartoons available here.

NICKELODEON PROPERTIES

Nickelodeon owns several channels and either produces or owns the right to show many different cartoons. Most of the cartoons tend to be rated TV-Y or TV-Y7. Many of these programs will be of interest to everyone, being (for the most part) aimed at children 7 and older. There is a mixture of long-running and more ephemeral cartoons.

STAR WARS

There have been several different groupings of cartoons that fit within the *Star Wars* canon. So far these cartoons have been rated TV-PG. While more mature than most of the cartoons previously mentioned, it is still completely appropriate for tweens.

Parent Nostalgia Cartoons

Many parents and grandparents have fond memories of Saturday morning cartoons or watching cartoons when they got home from school. It is hard not to smile when excited adults are exclaiming about finding cartoons from their young days in the tween area!

ANIMANIACS

This is a TV-Y7 series that aired during the 1990s. The show was quite popular at that time, and it still is funny for tweens today.

DUNGEONS AND DRAGONS

Yes, there was a short-lived animated series for Saturday morning television loosely based on the role-playing game of the same name. This program is on the list to let people know that both long-running and cult classic cartoons are currently more prevalent in DVD form.

FLINTSTONES

This Hanna-Barbera classic from the 1960s is a cartoon for both tweens' parents and their grandparents. There are quite a few Hanna-Barbera programs available on DVD. These cartoons from over fifty years ago are still funny today.

HE-MAN AND THE MASTERS OF THE UNIVERSE

This show has a rating of TV-Y7. It was a staple of the 1980s. Remember that parents often want to show their tweens these cartoons, or else their tweens provide an excuse for them to watch the television shows of their youth.

Anime

Finding appropriate tween anime is sometimes a challenge. As a general rule of thumb, go first to anime that was broadcast on Cartoon Network as part of the Toonami time block during the early to mid–2000s. These shows will be sanitized and edited versions of the original anime. Shows made in the anime style are also seen on Nickelodeon currently, and they used to be available on UPN and the WB when those stations were still around. These programs tended to carry a rating of TV-Y7.

The challenge is that many tweens may easily come across the Adult Swim anime playing on Cartoon Network late in the evenings. These shows are played at that time for a reason: they are not appropriate for tweens. Sometimes adults who are not familiar with anime do not realize that the storylines and visual depictions in these "cartoons" are frequently not appropriate for tweens. Many adults see a cartoon as a cartoon, but not all cartoons are for kids. As librarians, we certainly need to take the opportunity (when it presents itself) to educate parents and tweens about this particular story-telling format.

Hayao Miyazaki

Miyazaki is a very influential Japanese animator and film director, among other things. A number of the movies he has been involved in came through Studio Ghibli, which has a relationship with Disney. Many of Miyazaki's full-length anime movies are appropriate for tweens and are of interest to a wide range of ages. However, the films tend to be rated either G or PG.

Korean-style anime

While most anime is produced in Japan, there are several other countries, including Korea, with artist studios that produce high-quality anime, both for Korean productions and for movie studios worldwide. *Avatar: The Last Airbender* and *The Legend of Korra* are done in this style.

Pokémon

This program is usually rating TV-Y7. There has been at least one incarnation of the Pokémon franchise that was rated TV-Y, but, for the most part, this anime will be of interest to tweens, particularly those who play either the card or the handheld games.

Yu-Gi-Oh!

This anime has a lot in common with Pokémon. It is rated TV-Y7 and comes with a card game. It is also primarily, but not exclusively, the province of tweens.

Video Games

The first question may be: Does the library already circulate video games? Does it *want* to circulate video games? There are plenty of franchises producing many different titles that are all great for tweens. This age group loves to play video games. Games are interactive and can be played with friends. Tweens can show their skills and abilities in successfully completing the game.

There are a number of things to keep in mind if the tween area specifically, or the library in general, is going include video games as part of the tween AV collection.

- *Check the ratings*—All games have a rating. Games rated E and E10 are appropriate for tweens. The E rating means it is appropriate for everyone. Another way to look at it is that E games are ones the entire family can play together. E10 games will have some violence, usually characters fighting one another; there could also be some raw language or innuendos. However, none of these things are of the magnitude found in a title rated T (Teen).
- *Be conscious of the platform*—There are three main consoles: Wii, Xbox, and Playstation. The most recent versions are WiiU, Xbox One, and Playstation 4. However, there may be a number of patrons who are still using the previous platforms (that is, the Wii, Xbox 360, and Playstation 3). While these people cannot play games produced for the newer consoles, the newer consoles can still play the older games; they are backward compatible. Regarding handheld games, the Nintendo DS is still far and away the most popular. The Nintendo 3DS is the newest platform, but many children and even young tweens may be playing with a hand-me-down Nintendo DS.
- *Be aware of the intended audience of different platforms*—There is nothing that says a particular person must have one specific gaming system or another. However, some systems and their attendant games are marketed to specific clientele.
  - Xbox and Playstation tend to be marketed to teenage or adult males. This is not to say that females or families with small children cannot have these systems. However, more titles are produced for these systems with T (Teen) or more commonly M (Mature) ratings.
  - Wii tends to be marketed to families, with a large number of titles appropriate for families with different-aged children. There are even titles that cater specifically to girls. This system, more than the first two, is really great for tweens.
  - Nintendo DS is also a young system, and one that is often specifically marketed to girls. There are DS games advertised in girl-focused magazines. While there are plenty of titles that are interesting to boys, there is a definite subset of games that appeal to just girls.

It is helpful, as always, to remember that each library and each community will have different ideas about what is appropriate.

Cross-Platform Titles

When considering available video game titles, it is easier to look at franchises and specific types of games. The first grouping includes games that are available on at least two of the three major platforms.

- Adventure Time—These titles correspond to the cartoon of the same name on Cartoon Network and are rated E10.
- Disney games—In general, all Disney titles cross platforms, which is beneficial for libraries. These titles tend to be either E or E10.
- *Disney Infinity*—These games, which also have figurines that increase the inter-activity and level of play, are rated E10. Because the figurines are essential to the game, but are not easily circulated, these games may not be the best choices for the collection. However, it is worth mentioning them anyway because a tween may ask about these games, and there needs to be a reason why they are (or are not) available to borrow.
- Driving games—These are rated E, for everyone, and they are very popular with tweens. Not only can tweens compete with friends or family, but the tweens are also able to start "driving" before they are 16.
- *Guitar Hero*—These games are played on the older consoles, and they definitely have tween appeal in the sense of "I saw my older brother/sister/cousin/neigh-bor play this back in the day, and I want to as well." However, keep in mind these games are rated T, mainly due to some of the song lyrics. Libraries and librarians must decide if this is going to be a problem for the community.
- *Just Dance*—This can be an interesting franchise because sometimes the games are rated T, and other times there are specialized titles that are rated E. How-ever, the reason for the T rating usually has to do with the song lyrics. Depend-ing on what the community is like, there may be no problem with having these titles in the tween area.
- *LEGO*—This franchise has so many different titles. Generally all the games are rated E10. It would be best to have one of every title available for each of the three consoles. These tend to circulate really well. With LEGO's continued popularity, these games are solid choices for the tween area.
- Nickelodeon games—These are going to be titles based on television shows from the Nickelodeon channel; they tend to be rated either E or E10.
- *Plants vs. Zombies*—This franchise tends to be rated E10 and has a lot of tween appeal.
- *Rockband*—This game is similar to *Guitar Hero* in that it is an older game and one that is rated T due to song lyrics.
- *Skylanders*—This franchise is similar to *Disney Infinity* because the games are enhanced through the use of different figurines. As mentioned earlier, the need for figurines to fully enjoy the game could mean that *Skylanders* is not a good addition for the library collection.
- *Sonic*—Sonic the Hedgehog has been around for quite a while, with games on different consoles and different versions of consoles. Games featuring this character tend to be rated E.
- Sports titles—There are quite a few video games about sports that release annual editions. All are rated E, except the hockey games (which are rated

E10). These games have great tween appeal, but they are fine to play with families that include younger siblings. Librarians would do well to have a copy of every sport and get the new year's offerings when they come out.

- *Transformers*—Even though the movies were released a while ago, there are still great E10-rated games coming from this franchise.

Single-Platform Titles

There are some games that are only available for one console, and predominately that console is the Wii or WiiU.

- *Bomberman*—This is an E title that is just for the Wii. Tweens love playing it.
- Classic Nintendo games—These are titles that simulate games from early Nintendo consoles. Since they are rated E, everyone can play them.
- Donkey Kong—This character is originally from the Mario franchise, but he has his own games. This is rated E (for everyone).
- Kirby—There are both E and E10 titles for this character. Regardless, Kirby is a favorite with tweens.
- *Little Big Planet*—This is the only popular single-platform game for tweens that is not a Wii or WiiU title. This franchise is solely for the PlayStation. The games are rated E.
- Mario—He is the quintessential Nintendo character. The games in which Mario is the main focus are rated E.
- *Nintendo Land*—This is an E10 title, and very popular with tweens.
- *Super Smash Bros.*—This title for the Wii is rated T (for teen), since it has cartoon violence. However, many tweens enjoy playing it, so it may be worthwhile to keep a copy in the tween area.
- *Super Smash Bros. WiiU*—This incarnation of the game is rated E10, and there is no doubt that it belongs in the tween area.
- Yoshi—This character got its start with Mario for Nintendo, but it has its own E-rated titles.
- Zelda—This character has different games for Nintendo that are all rated E10.

Games for the Nintendo 3DS and DS

Since the Nintendo DS is a handheld device, it has been kept separate from the sections on the three consoles. While the DS is a Nintendo product, just as the Wii and WiiU are, it is very different. Generally the ratings for the franchises will be the same for the DS versions as for the console games. Many of the single-platform titles or franchises are the same on the DS, since the company is the same. However, it is worth calling attention to two titles that are special on the DS:

- Pokémon—These E-rated titles seem like the quintessential DS and 3DS franchise. While tending to appeal most to tween boys, anything connected to Pokémon is a definitely "must-get" item if the library plans to circulate DS games.
- *Star Wars*—Other than the LEGO *Star Wars* games, there are no *Star Wars* console titles that are appropriate for tweens. However, there are some DS titles in this franchise that are rated E10.

The Takeaway

There are many different types of AV materials to consider for the tween department. Remember, talk to tweens in the library to figure out what is best for the community. They will make suggestions and not hold back. Then the librarian must turn their suggestions into a reality.

AV materials include music, movies, television shows, and video games. Community standards can vary. Take the time to understand what all the options are and what types of content ratings already exist. Looking at things in discrete components can sometimes make it easier to understand all that is available to the library.

Tween AV materials can be described as:

- physical materials to borrow from the library;
- items that often have ratings associated with them;
- older CDs;
- DVDs that are currently popular with tweens;
- nostalgia movies and television (mostly for the benefit of parents and grandparents); and
- video games with either E or E10 ratings.

SECTION VI

The Continuum of Youth Programming

Before looking at programming specifically intended for tweens, it is time to consider in more detail programming for other youth groups in the library. It has been said throughout this book that youth programming is a continuum, and every stop on the continuum is important. This section focuses specifically on programming. Providing a range of materials is something libraries have been doing for years, but when it comes to programming, sometimes it is not a smooth transition when moving from activities for one age to those intended for another.

In libraries it is possible to be employed as a tween librarian while also serving in another library position. In this case, being two things at once may help you manage the continuum of programming in the library. However, it can be a balancing act to provide a comparable amount and variety of programming to different audiences. Unfortunately, it is human nature to give one group or another a little bit of an advantage, but being aware that you may have a bias toward a particular age range may help keep preferential treatment to a minimum.

The first chapter in this section is all about programs for children (i.e., birth through third grade). Within that very wide age range there are a lot of different activities going on. What is important about these programs, and why does it matter for tweens?

The second chapter looks at programming for young adults (used here as an umbrella term for teens and "new adults," which seems to be a term slowly gaining prominence as the descriptor for people ages approximately 19–30). One might think that since young adults are older than tweens, their programming wouldn't have any bearing on tween activities, but the continuum is critical because libraries want to create patrons for life. It is not good for long-term library health to have patrons disappear at some point during middle school or high school, never to return again.

These chapters will lay the groundwork for the section devoted to programming for tweens. Without a framework from which to view tween programming, it is harder to gain a solid understanding of how or what to provide for this difficult-to-describe group of people.

17

Library Services for Children

Tween services fit within the successful continuum of services that the library provides for youths of all ages in the same way that tween materials fit between materials for children and those for young adults. In the case of children's services and programming, it is all about being the foundation that tween services is built upon. Is there a strong foundation? If not, then there will be no buy-in or desire to continue in the library as tweens. Also, if there are great children's programs but nothing for tweens, these tweens will be lost and probably will not return. Without a successful base of children's programming, it is much more difficult to build successful tween programming.

Think about the library. Is there a lapsit or baby storytime? This is important for several reasons. In some communities, an activity for children under two or three years of age is fairly rare. If the library is within a community where there are stay-at-home parents or grandparents who are watching young children during the day, these people will welcome the opportunity to get out and see other adults for a little while. A big part of the benefit for the library in offering a baby program is that it will become a location where grown-ups can talk to other grown-ups or have a reason to take a shower and wear something other than sweatpants! Not only is the library providing a quality program, giving these babies a great foundation for literacy and learning, but giving the adults a chance to socialize is helpful too. If the adults are enjoying their time at the library's baby storytime, they will likely come back again with their babies. The other thing to consider with baby storytime is that the library may be "the only game in town" for that age child. Take advantage of that fact. Making sure that the library is part of as many families' lives as possible (and as soon as possible) helps the library's long-term sustainability.

At some point these children will transition to toddler storytime. This may also mean they are old enough for other activities in the community, perhaps dance or art classes, or even karate or swimming lessons. The two–to-three-year-old age range can mean that a new group of activities will become available to children and their attendant adults. As the library is building its toddler programs, it will be important to keep in mind what is going on in the community and, if possible, not plan programs at the same time. It is also important to keep in mind what time the local preschools dismiss, as well as kindergarten (if the community does part-day kindergarten). There may be caregivers who want to bring their child to the library's storytime but cannot because they have to pick up older children from school. By now the library staff should know many of these repeat-visit adults and can ask what they might be involved with in the community and how the library can make programming more effective and successful for them.

Those who will be providing tween services will have a vested interest in the success of their colleagues who offer children's programs; without successful children's programming, there will not be tweens in the library, and thus no one to provide tween services to. And unless the library is fortunate enough to be within a community where tweens can get to the library independently, tween librarians will need to have the support of parents, in the form of driving their tweens to the library. It is ideal to have parents who have brought their children to the library for years.

Preschool programming can be where a library starts to lose some of its regular program attendees. This is when being aware of the other programs happening in the community can come in handy. Children's programming should complement the other agencies in the community, not compete with them. Even if the library's program must be on the calendar at the same time that another group in town is doing something, at least acknowledge that in the planning. Continue to offer programs, even if some must be canceled because there are not enough attendees.

Another way to counteract, to a certain degree, the effects of losing some of the previously regular library attendees is preschool library outreach. Having a relationship with the community's preschools, and especially the ability to visit the preschools on a regular basis, is a way to maintain a relationship with the preschool children. Also, preschool is a good time for the tween librarian to start becoming aware of who will be "coming up" in a few years. Our suggestion is to "be around" when preschool storytime is going on at the library. Help the storytime leader if he/she needs assistance. Be a guest book reader. Assist with a special activity. Start getting your face seen by these children and their parents. Time goes quickly, and soon enough these children will be tweens.

When the core group of children whom the library has been cultivating and tending since they were babies reach kindergarten and the early elementary grades, more of them may disappear. At this time, weekly programs at the library could change to monthly activities or just special events. Sometimes that shift can be due to the library's staffing, but more often it is due to the activity level of the children. It bears repeating that reaching out and developing relationships with the other organizations in town is vital to avoid offering activities at competing times.

This is an opportune time to start diversifying your offerings. There can be science programs or book clubs, or perhaps LEGO programs or art activities. Also keep in mind that the library may be in a community where family activities are important. "Family" could mean early elementary children and their younger siblings. What types of events is the library holding that patrons of all ages can attend with their entire family?

The other question that comes with the young elementary groups is: How many children in a program is a good number? What does your library consider a successful program? It could be that baby storytime had 10–20 babies and their caregivers in the program, whereas the elementary-age book club has 5 students coming regularly. What is the threshold for a successful program to continue? Is it more successful to have passive programming or drop-in programming for this age group? Regardless, there is still a need for some sort of programming for the young elementary school students. Otherwise, why would the elementary school children still come to the library for activities?

There are two other aspects to library programming for children that are worth mentioning as they relate to tweens: the conundrum of being both a children's and a tween librarian as well as the challenge of transitioning from children's services to tween services.

Being a Children's and Tween Librarian

In an ideal world, a tween librarian only works with tweens, providing them with quality programming and materials. However, quite often tween librarians will split their time between tween services and children's services. Splitting time can be a challenge because there is a natural inclination to favor one group over another or to lump them together for simplicity's sake. Neither of these things is good. When one group seems favored with better programs or better times, the other group will feel like it is not worth coming to the library. And if too great an age spread is put into one program, the content is usually aimed at the youngest attendees, which will discourage older participants from coming.

If it turns out that tween services must be balanced with children's services, it will take conscious effort. Making sure that there are the same number of programs for each group is quite helpful. Are they varied in times or days of the week? Give everyone of both ages equal opportunities to attend programs. Sometimes it helps to check that the money spent on tweens and the money spent on children is comparable. Actually making a spreadsheet to track expenses is worth the time.

Transitioning to the Tween Section

It was mentioned much earlier in this book that assisting with children's programming can provide the children's services colleagues with much-appreciated help and allow the tween librarian to meet the soon-to-be tweens. Do not take this opportunity for granted. It is really beneficial, and not merely for the "bonding with colleagues" aspect. "Almost tweens" need to see whom they will work with next. It is not necessary to be front and center leading a program for children, but perhaps checking children in for a program will begin the process of getting to know their names. Likewise, going with the children's librarian for school outreach visits or to any outreach activities where there are children who will be tweens quite soon will be well worth your time. If the children's librarian includes the tween librarian in his or her program, that is an implicit endorsement of the tween librarian that both the children and their parents will see, whether they consciously acknowledge it or not.

The Takeaway

- Children's services lays the foundation for tween services.
- Good children's services are beneficial for the children and their adults.
- If a person is both the children's and the tween librarian, it is necessary to balance both areas as evenly as possible.
- It is important to meet tweens while they are children so they already know the tween librarian ahead of time.

18

Library Services for Teens
and New Adults

As was said at the beginning of this section, tween services fits within the continuum of services provided to library patrons of all ages. In the case of services for teens and new adults, sometimes lumped together as "young adults," tween services is the foundation that services for older youths are built upon. Children and tweens always want to be older than they are. Are there great teen programs that tweens want to attend? Are they attending the programs, or are services for the 15–30-year-old age range (using the largest age range possible) falling apart? Think about how these programs affect tweens. If there is not something interesting and exciting to anticipate and grow into at the library, then there is not as much incentive to participate in tween programs. Tweens will decide not to return to the library because it does not seem worthwhile. Again, to be successful with programming, the library must have a continuum of services for all ages.

Ideally there are young patrons who are attending tween programs and reading lots of books. In high school these youths can get lost to sports, afterschool clubs, jobs, and various other activities that are common at this age. As their time becomes filled with many more activities than they had when they were younger, what is the library doing to keep them coming back to the building? Are there interesting programs to attend? More important, what about the teens who graduate from high school but are living at home to attend college or trade school, or immediately entering the workforce? Many libraries drop these patrons like a hot potato once they graduate from high school. Now they are adults and can attend adult programs. However, many of these new adults still want the social aspects of the library activities they experienced in high school. And keep in mind, these eighteen-year-olds (and older) are now able to vote. If the library gets any sort of local funding that can somehow be related to voters choosing to fund the library, it is in the library's best interests to make sure these new voters will support the library at the polls. In addition, as if voting were not important enough, these teens and new adults will soon have children of their own. Ideally, if there are great teen and new adult programs keeping these patrons engaged in the library, then, once they have children, they will bring them to the library's baby storytime.

Just as the previous chapter featured a discussion of common programming for children at the library, there will be a similar discussion of common teen or new adult programming in the following pages. These are the things that tweens will want to grow into and be able to participate in when they are older. There are so many demands on the time of young adults, and they are also able to make many more of their own decisions. A baby or a toddler generally has no choice over whether he or she attends storytime at the library. It is a decision that the parents make. However, when these children grow up to be teens, they generally can choose whether they want to go to the library; it is not forced upon them. However, in order to be successful with programming for this age group, it is even more important to consider what is going on in the community at the same time so as not to compete with another entity.

When working with teens and new adults, the importance of outreach to schools is particularly noteworthy. Outreach can follow traditional patterns, like going into the school to conduct book-talks or promote a library program or service like summer reading. It can also be something more subtle like attending a football game, concert, or club fundraiser while wearing a shirt or jacket with the library logo on it. Helping with fundraisers and other school activities with parents of teens is a way to sell the library and keep it in teens' minds.

In the chapter about children's services, mention was made of diverse programming options, since preschool and early elementary school children will have lots of activities going on and start to develop new interests. At that age the idea is to offer different types of activities to attract different types of children. The same is true of teens and new adults. And it is also vital to know what might be more appropriate for one group versus the other.

Many libraries these days offer gaming programs for teens. These are frequently video games, but there are a growing number of board games and card games played as well. These games tend to be for older audiences. There can be *Super Smash Bros. Brawl* or, if they are older teens, games with slightly more mature content. For new adults, there can be tournaments using mature titles such as *Black Ops* or *Halo*.

"Doing" programs are always popular. Art-focused activities like henna art, scrapbooking, or painting attract many teens. The same can be done with new adults. There can be competition games in which there are short challenges of some kind to complete. These activities are popular, especially if there are prizes. Even new adults can be persuaded to participate in these game show–type competitions.

Themed events are also popular. Teens seem to enjoy "anti–Valentine's Day" activities, regardless of whether they have a significant other. Halloween is another popular celebration. Scary movie nights and game nights are both enjoyable options. New adults also come to game nights, but they have been known to do more activities with food or cooking as well.

Being a Tween and Teen Librarian

Just as tween librarians frequently have to double as children's librarians, they may also have to split their time between tween services and teen services, and sometimes even young adult services. This is a tremendously large age span in which many development changes occur. As before, one must avoid the temptation to privilege one group over another. When one group seems favored with better programs or better times, then the other group will feel that there is no point in coming to the library. The time and day conundrum is greater with tweens and teens because these groups have so many different activities going on all the time. It is also easy in this case to favor the teens over the tweens. By the time tweens have become teens, most of the huge swings in behavior and attitude that characterize the tween years have ended. While teens can be snarky and challenging, it is a different type of challenge than with tweens, leading many to prefer working with the older group.

The other danger is bringing both groups together into a single program, which runs the risk of content being aimed more at the younger participants (thus resulting in the older attendees losing interest). This is a more pronounced problem when it comes to combining tweens and teens because ordinarily tween programs are less complex or mature versions of teen programs. Teens want their own programs with more mature topics and activities; they do not want to be stuck in the same program with middle school students. And if there are any post–high school patrons coming to the programs, they really will not want to spend too much time with the middle school students (and possibly not even with the high school students)!

If it is necessary for one person to juggle tween and young adult librarian duties, make sure that there is the same number of programs available for each group. Ideally programs will be varied in times or days of the week, so as to provide as many opportunities as possible for those interested to attend. Keep an eye on the money spent for tween and teen programming, preferably using a spreadsheet to track expenses, so as to confirm that the amounts for both types of programming are comparable.

Transitioning from the Tween Section

It was mentioned much earlier that assisting with young adult programming can provide the young adult colleagues with much-appreciated help and also allow the tween librarian the opportunity to say good-bye to the former tweens. Do not take this opportunity for granted. At the same time, invite the young adult librarian to meet the soon-to-be teens by assisting with the tween programming. (Keeping with the idea of a continuum of library youth services, this mutual assistance will echo the relationship between those leading the children's programming and the tween librarian.) The young adult librarian does not have to lead a tween program, but even minor interactions such as checking tweens in for a program will allow the colleague to get to know names and faces. This is about collegial relations and being supportive of others. Inviting the young adult librarian to go on a school visit or other visits in the community is another great way to start bridging the tweens to the young adult stage.

The investment made in young adult services is worthwhile for several reasons.

One is giving an implicit endorsement of the young adult librarian to both the tweens and their parents, although it may not be consciously acknowledged. Second, helping out in young adult programs will create something of a safety net for the "newly teen," since those former tweens will know and be comfortable with the tween librarian. For the good of the library, tweens need to continue to grow and become active participants in the library as they mature.

The Takeaway

- Young adult services provides the interesting programs that a tween can attend once in high school.
- Good young adult services help soon-to-be voters remember why they are willing to give the library money during election season.
- If the tween and young adult librarian jobs are combined, it is necessary to balance both areas as evenly as possible.
- Helping tweens transition to teen services as well as giving the young adult librarian an opportunity to meet the tweens will help the overall library continuum.

SECTION VII

Tween Programming

There is more information available about tween programming than any other aspect of library services for tweens. There are articles in professional journals and at least one book just about programming. However, never forget that tweens in each community are unique, so it can be hard to look at someone else's ideas and know whether they will be similarly successful in another community. In this section, programming for tweens is examined—the successes and the "not quite successes." (It is important to discuss the "not quite successes" because they may provide successful programming ideas for another community.)

What are the potential components of successful tween programming? It is a recipe. Sample tween programs are provided, including both programs that were successful and some that were not. One must also consider what each library labels as "success." In talking with lots of different librarians who do programming for multiple age ranges, from children through senior citizens, it becomes clear that they measure success very differently. For some libraries, a program with four or five attendees is basically a failure. However, at another library four coming to a program is great. That program is a success!

The second chapter looks at the idea that "everything old is new again." In this day and age of social media and tweens being buried in their devices instead of verbally communicating with the person sitting next to them, there seems to be a lot of success with using activities from "long ago." The sad part is that "long ago" is any time prior to the dawn of the Internet. However, reaching back to one's childhood (or even that of one's parents) may yield some ideas for activities to do in the library with tweens.

Tween programming frequently is what gets tweens in the door who have not been to the library in a while, if ever. It is a critical piece of the overall concept of library services for tweens.

19

Recipes for Successful and Unsuccessful Tween Programs

Just as recipes have ingredients and steps to follow, so do tween programs. When cooking, there are fundamental techniques that are good to know before starting a recipe, and the same is true of tween programs: it helps to have some basic building blocks in place before starting to offer programs.

Is there a foolproof formula for guaranteed success in tween programming? No. However, community research will give tween librarians some help, as will working with their own tween advisory group. The other thing to remember is that if something does not work the first time, try it again. It is going to take at least two, if not three, tries before one can conclude that this particular idea is not working in the community. Giving up too soon can be more damaging than not trying at all.

There are some general characteristics that apply to tween programming. However, determining what an individual library views as a successful program is also important. There is nothing worse than creating what appears to be an amazing program and either having a supervisor say it cannot be done because it does not fit certain programming criteria or, worse yet, having no tweens show up.

Successful programming characteristics include the following:

- *Buzz*—Librarians cannot create buzz. They need other people to talk about what they are doing. Librarians want parents at the soccer field discussing it. They want tweens themselves asking their peers "Are you going to the library for ___?" The greater the number of shares on Facebook for a program announcement or the number of questions the circulation or reference staff are asked about an upcoming tween program, the better.
- *Interest*—This is something a librarian can have better control over, but interest will be generated more by the tween advisory group. Incorporating the advisory group's ideas will guarantee that what they think is cool and of the moment is part of what the library is doing. The advisory group will also create interest because they will announce to their friends that this program is their idea.
- *Attention to Detail*—This can mean a lot of different things, such as planning for

multiple eventualities and being ready for every potential situation or creating a high-action, high-interest program organized around a specific theme. Being attentive to detail can also mean making sure that a program is not competing with something else in the community for the same age group. Keeping track of what other groups are doing, especially if they work with tweens, will help a lot in providing programming that tweens will attend.

- *Supervision*—Depending on what the librarian is planning, he or she will need different levels of help. Sometimes it works really well to have two adults in the room; other times one is enough. Sometimes it is great if there is one male and one female supervisor. It may be helpful to have someone with a lot of "boss cred" to lend legitimacy to the event. It is also advisable to make sure that parents feel comfortable leaving their tweens with whomever is running the program. However, if there are library staff working with the tweens who demonstrate through words or actions that they do not like tweens but are merely putting in time, then the program is not going to be successful.

- *An Experience*—Tweens have so many demands on their time. What will make a library program an experience worth having? It is going to be something different from what is currently happening elsewhere in the community. It is also an opportunity for tweens to socialize. There has to be time for talking and relating and interacting in an environment that is not school. Is it going to be something that allows tweens to differentiate themselves as those who did and those who did not participate?

- *Structured versus Unstructured*—The term "unstructured structure" has been used in the realms of fashion and architecture, but it does not have a specific meaning. However, in the context of tween library programs it means building in time when there is not a specific plan for what to do. (It could be argued, though, that planning not to have a plan is actually a plan.) Many tweens are very regimented, and they have to be in order to accomplish all the varied things they do. However, sometimes what the library can provide is an opportunity for planned "downtime." It is a time to be able to do whatever they want—within reason, of course!

There are many characteristics of successful programs for youths of all ages that also apply to tween programs.

- *Planning for success, not failure*—Generally people plan for failure in library programs instead of success. However, when a program is an unanticipated success, it can be a bigger problem than a failure. Planning for success is an art form, and it is hard because planning for failure also means keeping expenses to a minimum. Although preparing for the worst may seem like the wisest thing to do, in fact it can sometimes mean, to follow the cliché, "cutting off your nose to spite your face." Perhaps the best way to look at this is that if, after planning for success, consumables are left over, it means the program can be repeated because it was successful and people enjoyed it.

- *Taking advantage of what the library has available*—The library has books. Perhaps the tween librarian might organize a program centered around a specific character or book. The program will not necessarily involve reading the book, but rather celebrating some element of the book (or books). Movies or music can be used in a similar way; there could be an event celebrating the opening of a particular movie or its arrival on DVD for borrowing. Celebrating what a library does well and using it to best advantage is a way to build a successful program. However, what a library also can have is space. Do not underestimate the potential for the library to serve as a neutral location for people of similar interests to gather.

- *Being flexible*—It is impossible to know how a group of people will behave together, regardless of their age. This issue tends to be more prevalent with tweens because they can cover such a wide developmental range. Adjusting for a group of predominately older or younger tweens is something that a librarian must do in the moment depending on the makeup of a particular program. The ability to adjust to the conditions of the moment is crucial. It can mean changing the order of activities or even deciding not to do something that was planned if conditions suggest that it would not be a good idea.

- *Engaging with broad topics and wide age ranges*—Sometimes there are programs that can allow a wide range of ages to mix together. This is not about the parent who keeps trying to put the older or younger sibling into the program with his or her correctly aged sibling so that both will be entertained at the same time. Instead, this is about making use of a common topic of interest, such as *Harry Potter*. Lots of people, from elementary school children to adults, are interested in the *Harry Potter* series and any activities that replicate elements of the books, no matter how childish they might seem. Video game tournaments can also be a multi-age activity depending on the game chosen. Young children and tweens can happily compete in a *Mario Kart* tournament while tweens and young adults can both participate in a *Super Smash Bros.* tournament.

- *Encouraging creativity*—Being open to the suggestions and interests of the community can mean having lots of different, inventive programming that appeals to many different segments of the library service population. It is impossible to predict what someone might suggest, and it is similarly impossible to know what might spark people's interest.

Programming for tweens is a moving target. Therefore, having some ideas to start with can really help. However, as has been continually said, research about a particular community will help librarians find good programs. Please keep in mind that what has been described as successful or not quite successful here may be exactly the opposite for another librarian. Think of this as a list of suggestions to consider or bring up with the tween advisory board.

Each program discussed below will be treated like a recipe. The "ingredients" will be listed first, then general procedures/instructions, and finally the commentary about the program. The first list will detail programs attempted at various libraries that were ultimately not as successful as the programmers hoped.

Storytelling

Ingredients

- stories from different folktale or "scary stories" books from the library, like Alvin Schwartz's *Scary Stories to Tell in the Dark*

Procedures

1. Read the stories enough ahead of time to be able to tell them from memory.
2. Turn off all lights and draw the blinds so the space is as dark as possible.
3. Illuminate the storyteller with only a flashlight or else stand under a black light.
4. Tell the stories to tweens.
5. Wait for the applause to thunder.

Commentary

This program will work in some communities and not in others. Places where there are strong oral traditions and histories of sharing stories will find success with this program. However, in hindsight, this may not work as the sole or main activity for tweens, as it is too sedentary and does not have enough audience participation.

CCG Day (Collectible Card Game Day)

Ingredients

- tweens with Pokémon, Yu-Gi-Oh!, or Magic the Gathering cards
- an adult library staff member who knows the rules of the game(s)

Procedures

1. Announce that tweens who have Pokémon, Yu-Gi-Oh!, or Magic the Gathering cards can come to the library to play the card game with other people who have cards.
2. Have lots of people show up to play.
3. A staff member officiates the games and referees disputes over rules and orders of operations.
4. Everyone leaves happy.

Commentary

There was not enough specific information shared or directions given in advance of this program. It would have been helpful to specify that people should know the rules of Pokémon or similar games ahead of time. Some who came to this event knew the rules and were very serious about playing. Others were more interested in the cards themselves and trading them but didn't seem interested in playing the games by the stated rules. Neither group had fun. Each was looking for something completely different out of the event. However, the success of this type of program will be directly related to a particular library's group of tweens. It may work perfectly in one place and fail in another library ten miles away.

Dance

Ingredients

- a DJ
- snacks and drinks

Procedures

1. Get a DJ to handle music.
2. Have the tweens come and dance.
3. Feed the attendees and give them something to drink when they need it.
4. Have everyone think the library is awesome for hosting a dance.

Commentary

This is an example of program saturation. If other community groups are holding similar activities, it is probably not one that should be done at the library. There was a lot of "clumping in corners" that happened at this event, followed by questions about when something else was going to happen. It did not fit with other successful library activities.

Nintendo DS Meet-ups

Ingredients

- library Wi-Fi access
- kids with their own Nintendo DS
- at least one copy of *Mario Kart* for the Nintendo DS

Procedures

1. Make sure there is a staff person on hand who understands how to get every tween's DS onto the library Wi-Fi.
2. Have one tween use the *Mario Kart* cartridge so everyone can play.
3. Enjoy a quiet and successful library program.

Commentary

When this program was offered, there were some tweens who came, but not enough to make it a continuing event. It is a victim of the parameters describing a successful program (i.e., the number of people who must attend for the program to be considered a success).

Halloween

Ingredients

- costume contest
- "minute to win it" games
- scary story to read
- gross things to touch

Procedures

1. Plan and set up the competitions, like knocking over bowling pins with a baseball stuffed into the leg of a pair of pantyhose or picking up Life Savers with a piece of spaghetti held in one's mouth.
2. Welcome the tweens, who have a wonderful time playing games and guessing what the gross things they touched actually are.

3. Share a short scary story from an anthology.
4. Give prizes for the most creative costumes.

Commentary

Sometimes themes, like Halloween, that are successful with younger children, drawing huge numbers, are not as effective for tweens. This is another example of theme and/or activity saturation in the community.

Mardi Gras

Ingredients

- "minute to win it" games
- multicolored plastic beads

Procedures

1. Get everything ready for the games.
2. Give people a strand of beads for successfully completing each game.

Commentary

It seems like a great idea: Have a party. Play games. Win prizes. But hardly anyone came to this event. There were too many things going on at the time—sports practices, homework, church activities. This is another example of what can result from not consulting the list of the community's events.

Movies

Ingredients

- movie license
- Blu-rays or DVDs of movies that are licensed to show in public
- popcorn
- soda

Procedures

1. Find movies that have just been released on DVD.
2. Check to see which of these movies the movie license covers.
3. Show the movie, serving popcorn and soda to those who come to watch.

Commentary

Movies are fine as background noise for another activity, and they work well as part of a larger program. But most people do not come to the library just to see a movie—or at least not in large enough numbers to make movie viewing a sustainable program. However, for some libraries, this program works well and is quite popular.

Fortunately, there are many more successful programs than unsuccessful ones, although this is once again a matter of opinion. What works for one library may not work somewhere else—that is the challenge with tween programming. It is a moving target that is less stable and replicable than children's or young adult programming, but it is still worth doing.

Pie Fight

Ingredients

- lots of containers of generic whipped cream (brand-name products are too expensive)
- disposable pie dishes
- the largest cooler available
- a raincoat and set of pants for each adult supervisor
- sprinkler head
- hose hooked up to an outside faucet

Procedures

1. Purchase enough whipped topping for two pie dishes per tween signed up.
2. Keep everything in the cooler so it does not liquefy.
3. Give each tween his or her first pie dish.
4. Let them fling the whipped cream pies at friends, adults, or whatever else they like.
5. Repeat with the second set of dishes.
6. Have the participants run through the sprinkler to clean off the whipped topping.

Commentary

Calling this event a "pie fight" is using the term loosely; this really was chucking handfuls of whipped cream at each other in the yard of the library. What is important about this idea is that it came from the tween advisory group as the result of a brainstorming session about activities that could be related to food. At first this seemed impossible, but eventually, in talking with the tweens, it turned out that the idea of flinging gobs of whipped cream at each other and then running through a sprinkler afterward to clean off seemed like a lot of fun to them. So that is what happened.

Strange Foods

Ingredients

- barbecue, salt and vinegar, and cheddar cheese crickets
- cheddar cheese and salt and vinegar mealworms
- food from a semi-local ethnic markets, such as Korean, Chinese, and Middle Eastern

Procedures

1. Decide the budget for "strange foods" and spend accordingly. Purchasing the most unusual food possible will work best.
2. Prepare small tastes of the different offerings.
3. Let the tweens taste the food and give each dish a rating.
4. Give the leftover food to the tweens to take home to give to their families.

Commentary

There have been several programs that fall under this basic description. One time tweens ate bugs, and only bugs, from the local candy store. Another time they tasted delicacies from other countries and cultures. Both events were amazingly successful and proved to be fodder for conversations and parental Facebook posts for days afterward.

Any Food Program

Ingredients

- different foods, as fits your theme

Procedures (these will vary based on what is done)

1. Set aside almost twice the preparation time as you think it should take.
2. Set your budget so as not to overspend and decide what will happen with the food leftovers before holding the event.

Commentary

"Strange foods" have a certain cachet as far as being able to tell another tween, "I ate a cricket. Where were you?" These days seemingly anything having to do with making food or taking part in the process of creating food can be successful. One might also try a chocolate fountain program, or "make your own pizzas," or "make your own gummy candy," to name a few. While allergies are still a source of concern (even if the kids are less concerned about their allergies than their parents would like them to be), these are still very successful activities. Experiment with different ideas, and, of course, have the tween advisory board give suggestions.

Touch Boxes

Ingredients

- items like apricots, nori, spring roll wrappers, whole canned tomatoes, marshmallows, and corn nuts
- boxes with openings large enough to stick a hand inside

Procedures

1. Although it is possible to buy "touch boxes," they can also be made from scratch; they should be painted black and the openings covered with black craft foam so tweens cannot look inside.
2. Prepare the food items.
3. Label the boxes with unreal descriptions like "zombie skin" or "intestines."
4. Let the tweens touch the items inside the boxes and write down what they think they actually are.
5. Clean and dry the boxes thoroughly after the program if they will be reused.

Commentary

It is easy to envision the "reach your hand in and touch something disgusting" activity that has been a common Halloween party theme. That is basically what this is, but it does not have to be reserved for Halloween. It has been done at other times as part of programs that involved testing and experimenting, as well as different food programs. This activity is mentioned separate from Halloween because it has seemed to work best then.

LEGO Club

Ingredients

- LEGO-obsessed tweens bringing in creations from home
- an adult supervisor
- ideas for "build offs"

Procedures

1. Advertise the group as being for LEGO aficionados.
2. Recruit a tween to run the program.
3. Have an adult in the room during the program to handle any rambunctious kids or provide prodding to the tween running the program if necessary.

Commentary

This is an interesting activity because in its current iteration it is starting to wane, but it has been a successful program for a while. The original idea came from a member of the tween advisory group; instead of coming to the library to build LEGOs, he wanted people to bring their already-built creations. It was an interesting idea, and while the original participants are no longer interested in LEGOs, many are in high school (or almost there), so it is an example of a grassroots program.

Live Pac-Man

Ingredients

- several hundred one-inch-diameter Styrofoam balls
- 4 five–six-inch-diameter topiary balls
- 5 XXL colored T-shirts, matching the colors of Pac-man and the four ghosts (Inky, Pinky, Blinky, and Clyde)
- a tote bag

Procedures

1. It is an investment to buy so many supplies—plan ahead.
2. Purchase the items.
3. On the day of the event, spread the Styrofoam balls throughout the aisles of the library where the program is taking place to mimic the pathways traveled by Pac-man in the old video and arcade game.

4. Intersperse the topiary balls, functioning as power pellets from the original game, throughout the pathway.
5. Choose 1 Pac-man and 4 ghosts, and give each an appropriate colored shirt to wear.
6. Allow other attendees to watch from around the area of play (but not in the way!).
7. Let the ghosts go into the play area and arrange themselves throughout.
8. Send Pac-man into the play area. He must pick up power pellets as he goes and try to avoid the ghosts who are after him.
9. If Pac-man gets a power pellet, he can chase after a ghost and try to tag him/her.
10. Play ends when Pac-man has been tagged by a ghost or picks up all the Styrofoam balls in the area of play.
11. Return the Styrofoam balls and the power pellets to the game area to set up for the next group of five players.
12. Keep repeating until everyone has had a chance to play.
13. A winner is selected based on who had the most Styrofoam balls in the bag when he was tagged by a ghost.

Commentary

This program was also a suggestion from the advisory group. One young man decided that the shelves reminded him of the pathways that Pac-Man travels along, and after some brainstorming and sketching, the game took shape. It has been taken on the road to other locations, where it has been played in a field instead of the aisles of the library. This game is a testament to the power of suggestions from the advisory group. (In this same vein, there is information online about librarians doing live *Clue*, *Candy Land*, and *Hungry, Hungry Hippos*.)

Lock-Ins

Ingredients

- vast quantities of pizza
- 5 gallon beverage containers
- economy-size powdered drink mixes
- cups, plates, and napkins
- library resources such as computers, video game systems, board games, DVDs, etc.
- one flashlight per tween
- sneakers on tweens' feet
- at least three adult chaperones there for at least three quarters of the event

Procedures

1. Publicize the upcoming lock-in beginning at 7:30 p.m. Friday and ending at 7:30 a.m. Saturday; be sure to mention that there is no expectation of sleep during the 12-hour program.
2. Have a guardian sign a permission slip in person at the library in advance of the event.
3. Pre-order pizza with local pizzeria because a lot is needed. It will be the only food.
4. Check in tweens when they come and verify that they have sneakers on.
5. Go over the rules of the evening so the tweens understand what to expect.
6. Play "old-school" games outside for the first hour to hour and a half.
7. Eat pizza.
8. Play flashlight tag, infection, sardines, or simply hide and seek for about an hour.
9. Turn the tweens loose to the other activities available to them through the library.
10. About 2:30 a.m., have everyone play another group game. It will probably be one of the games played earlier in the event.
11. Have adults come in and sign for the tweens when it is pick-up time so as to verify that everyone has left.

Commentary

It takes a lot of staff energy and commitment to pull off this event, but it has become one of the most successful tween programs; its success comes from indulging tweens' desire to structure their own time and simply be kids. However, the commitments of tweens and their families during the weekend (sports, Scouts, and school-related activities for either the tweens or their parents) are making it harder for them to participate if they must do something else later in the weekend. The other thing to note is that there will be fewer potential behavior problems if the lock-in happens on a Friday when there has been no school (this can be during the school year or in the summer), as the tweens will be more well rested before the event ever starts.

The Takeaway

Consider the ideas detailed on the preceding pages suggestions. There are no guarantees that they will or will not work for another library. Run them past the tween advisory group, and see what they think.

- Remember that good programs for tweens will need to incorporate flexibility, creativity, and planning for success.

Section VII. Tween Programming

- Using the suggestions and assistance of the tween advisory board increases the likelihood of program success.
- Food programs will be popular for most libraries.
- It is possible to do an all-night lock-in with tweens, though it will take much planning and preparation.

20

Everything Old Is New Again

It is an interesting phenomenon that librarians have been noticing for a while: things that seem "old-fashioned" are popular with tweens today. Keep in mind that *old-fashioned* means anything that was popular before the dawn of the Internet in the mid–1990s. There are some activities that seem so simplistic that it is surprising that media-engrossed, information-saturated tweens get excited about participating in them. Or there is the astonishment of adults finding out that many tweens have not done some of the things they believe "everyone does." Bear in mind that different communities of tweens will embrace "the old" to varying degrees. For some, there will be a lot of interest in "old stuff," but for others there may only be mild or moderate interest.

This chapter is meant to help librarians realize that they may have more programming possibilities than they initially thought. It is easy to get carried away with the idea that programs need to have lots of shiny, flashing pieces, which usually cost money. However, there are more librarians asking "how do I do programs on the cheap?" than librarians with endless resources. Librarians can think about what they enjoyed as tweens. More than likely there will be tweens who like the same things today. Do not be fooled into thinking that the tweens seen in the library will always be buried in their tablets and phones; given the right enticement, they will put those devices down. Do not limit the programming options, and as the possibilities of "retro" activities are explored, check with the tween advisory board. It could be surprising what they suggest as "retro" or enthusiastically endorse.

Board Games

Rather than the complicated role-playing board games that are coming to prominence for young adults and adults, this category encompasses classic board games like *Life, Monopoly, Sorry, Connect Four, Battleship, Clue,* and even *Candy Land,* to name a few. Games that seem simple and common to a generation of librarians who grew up playing them are interesting and fun to tweens today. Of course, classic games are classics for a reason, but the tweens really have a good time playing them. There is no research to back up these claims. However, the laughing and gathering in tight groups around the game board cannot be disputed.

Please note that chess and checkers are being kept separate from these other board games even though they are technically the same. Some libraries have chess clubs or chess and checkers groups already. Frequently these games are thought of as the province of adults. However, there are tweens playing both of these games, particularly chess. Many upper elementary school teachers have taught their students chess in class for various reasons. As a result, these tweens are interested in playing with anyone who is willing, and the library can fill that role.

Card Games

Much of the time tweens are seen playing more contemporary card games like Pokémon, Yu-Gi-Oh!, and even Magic the Gathering. However, sitting and playing traditional card games for hours is not uncommon. Working together to teach new players the rules can be an everyday occurrence. There are also those tweens who are excited to show that they know how to play games with a regular pack of cards. Watching the tweens play can be quite funny because they are so proud of themselves, and frequently they actually do not know all the rules! Here are a few card games to teach tweens (the rules are included). Having some packs of standard playing cards in the tween area is not a bad idea. It is impossible to know when it might be a good time for some card games.

Go Fish!

Many tweens will have played this game as young children using cards sporting different types of fish. However, using a deck of regular playing cards can seem grown-up and very different from their "childhood game." This game is best with four people. To start, the deck is shuffled, and each person gets five cards. The rest of the cards are put face down in a pile. The idea is to collect four of a kind—the same number or face card, with one from each of the four suits of cards. The player going first asks someone else if he has a particular card (say, the two of spades). If that player has the card, he gives it to the player who asks. If he does not, he tells the asking player to "Go Fish." The first player then takes the top card from the pile and keeps it in his hand. Play moves to the left, and each player takes turns asking someone else for a card, either receiving the card thus requested or choosing one from the pile. As four of a kind are achieved, they are laid down on the table in front of the player. The game ends when one player no longer has cards in his hand. The winner will be the player with the most groups of four on the table.

I Doubt It

Among adults this game may be known by a different name, but "Bull sh*t" is not appropriate language to be used repeatedly in the library by anyone, especially tweens! However, tweens do love the idea of bluffing with their friends. The nice thing is that there can be almost as many players as anyone would like for this game, so long as there are at least three. The winner is the person who gets rid of all his cards first. In this game the cards are shuffled and dealt face down to all the players until all the cards are gone. The person going first must put down an ace. He can declare that he is putting down one, two, three, or four aces face down in the center of the table. However, what he actually puts down may not be what he declares it is. Any player may say "I doubt it" after the declaring person puts down the cards if he or she believes that what is placed on the pile is not correct. When the cards are turned over, if the declaring person bluffed and put other cards down, then that person has to take back the entire pile and put it in his or her hand. If, however, the declaring person truly put down the cards he or she declared, then the person who said "I doubt it" has to take the pile of cards. Play continues, going through the numbers and face cards until it returns to aces again, and the number sequence repeats itself. The game ends when one player has no cards left.

War

This is a two-person card game played with a standard deck of cards. The winner is the person who ultimately ends up with all the cards. The deck is shuffled and dealt one card to each player until all the cards are dealt face down into two piles. Then each player turns over his top card. The player with the higher value of the two cards gets to keep both of them, which go to the bottom of his pile. (In this game, aces are the highest value card.) Play continues like this until the two players turn over a card of the same value. At that point they "declare war." Each player takes the top three cards from his pile and leaves them face down. They then take a fourth card and turn that face up. The player with the highest value card gets to keep all eight cards. If the face-up cards in the war are of the same value, there is a "double war," meaning a second drawing of three cards face down and a fourth one turned up. At that time the player with the highest value card turned over gets to keep all sixteen cards. Play then continues as normal until one player has no cards left.

Video Games

It may seem odd to include video games in a chapter about "old things." However, to tweens, video games that were popular with their older siblings five or more years ago *are* old games. Things like *Guitar Hero* or *Rock Band* (the pieces of which are hard to find these days) are fun to play because they are retro games to these kids. It is fun to show off skills with older games to one's friends. The same can be said of playing earlier versions of *Super Mario Bros.* Knowing where all the hidden Easter eggs are when playing with a group gives tweens an opportunity to show off for their peers.

Remember that video game systems have been around since the 1980s, and there are some parents of tweens who jealously guard their original Atari, Nintendo 64, Sega Genesis, and other systems. Even though by today's standards the early games are primitive, tweens still enjoy playing them. It is possible to use emulators and other equipment to get the these retro games to play on newer consoles. There is probably a tween or a tween's family who knows the technical requirements for the librarian to do this in the building. There are also current incarnations of retro games available for modern game systems; they are configured to play with current equipment, and tweens can spend hours engrossed in these games.

Running Games

Back in "the old days" in gym class, children learned how to play Mother May I, Red Rover, and many variations of tag. This is not to say that modern children are not learning these games at school or other places, but it seems like a large number of youths are not familiar with them these days. Holding programs in which these games are part of the activities can be an interesting adventure. Sometimes the tweens are willing and able to run for hours, playing these games and laughing. Sometimes they find the games juvenile and confusing, and they will not be bothered to put in much effort. These activities are different from the organized sports of rec leagues and school teams. There is no coach or captain. Tweens have to figure out how to complete these games, and sometimes the basketball star or the tween with lots of soccer talent is not great at these games!

Capture the Flag

There is something to be said for letting the tweens decide on the rules for this game themselves, which can sometimes make the game harder or easier than it might be ordinarily. It can also teach tweens some important social skills about getting along with people and behaving honorably in a group. Sometimes the game can be played with each team having a flag and guarding it, or there can be one team guarding a flag and one team trying to capture it. This is a popular game for tweens to decide on their own that they want to play during a library lock-in. Sometimes they can play for an hour or two, if they can agree to abide by the same set of rules. To play, it is necessary to have at least one flag or object that can be hidden. It can be a little banner on a stick or a sweatshirt that is not being worn. While the basic idea is either to keep one team's flag from being captured or to capture the other team's flag, how that happens is different in every game. Sometimes teams plan elaborate strategies, and other times the tweens just run around. However, an adult may need to officiate when it comes to agreeing on the boundary between the teams, how prisoners (people caught behind enemy lines) are released, how released prisoners get back to their own side, and whether the flag to be captured is allowed to be fully or only partially hidden. An online search confirms that there are many very specific variations of this game. It is best to allow the tweens to decide what rules they want to use and to only step in when it is absolutely necessary. No matter what version is chosen, the lessons the players learn in this game are priceless.

Darkened Room Hide and Seek

This game is still the classic hide and seek, but it's played in the dark environment of a library lock-in. This is not to say that regular hide and seek cannot be played at the library, but this activity is a staple of library lock-ins. If the area is pitch black, then participants need a flashlight. Some long-time lock-in players have even been known to convince their adult supervisors to buy headbands or something for their head that holds a light so they do not have to run and carry a flashlight in their hand. If the area is only semi-dark (because there are emergency lights on or something like that), then flashlights may not be necessary. It is important to make sure everyone knows where home base is and where they cannot go to hide. (These directions are usually given by adults.) Depending on how many people are playing, there can be multiple "its." A ratio of one "it" to every fifteen kids playing works best. Everyone hides, while the "its" close their eyes. After a few minutes they begin to count loudly from 50 to 1. Then the "its" start running. If a person who is "it" sees someone hiding, it is up to that person to get out from their hiding place and run. Basically they run until they are tagged or the "it" finds someone else to chase. Home base is generally where those who have been tagged go to wait for the next game to start. If a space is really dark, someone who is "it" can easily walk by a person who is hiding. The person only has to run if they do not want to be tagged by the person who is "it."

Freeze Tag

The timeless game of freeze tag is still quite fun for tweens to play. A large grassy area is preferred as the field of play. The important thing to establish at the beginning is whether "unfreezing" is allowed. Usually the game is played such that the person who is "it" must chase the other players, getting close enough to touch them; anyone tagged in this way must "freeze" in place. Most versions of freeze tag allow a frozen player to be unfrozen after being tapped by another player who is not frozen. However, it is also possible for people to stay frozen, and then the last person left unfrozen becomes "it" for the next game.

Infection

"Infection" has many names; it is also a version of tag. The idea is that one person begins as "it." All the other players run. As the "it" begins tagging people, they also become "it" and can tag people. The game ends when it appears that everyone has been infected. Another version of this game is zombie tag, where the first person who is "it" must hold their arms out in front of them and appear to move like a zombie while trying to tag people. As people get tagged, they also move like zombies. Because of the distinctive look, it is easier for players playing zombie tag to know who has been tagged and who is still available for capture.

Red Light, Green Light

While similar to Mother May I and other games where players can move for a period of time and then must stop, Red Light, Green Light is also a listening game. The idea is that the person calling the colors (usually another tween, but sometimes it can be one of the adults at the program) must stand with his back to the rest of the group. When "green light" is called, the players can move forward quickly. When "yellow light" is called, they are supposed to move slowly. For "red light," the caller turns around immediately to see if anyone is moving; those still in motion after "red light" is called are sent back to the beginning. Sometimes other colors like "purple light" or "maroon light" are called, which provide another opportunity to turn around and see if anyone is moving. The winner is the person who gets to the caller first.

Sardines

This game is yet another version hide and seek. It can be played in the dark (or, more accurately, semi-dark) of the library lock-in; dim lighting adds an interesting dimension to the game. The idea is that everyone except one person covers their eyes and counts. The one person not counting goes and hides somewhere. When the counting is finished, the other players search for this one person; when he or she is found, the seekers must also hide with them. Play continues until the hiding spot runs out of room or everyone playing has been fit in there. As with Darkened Room Hide and Seek, use a ratio of 1 to 15—that is, one hider for every fifteen people playing. This also means the hiding spots do not have to hold quite as many people.

Steal the Bacon

This game is a bit of a hybrid of tag and listening games like Red Light, Green Light. There are two sides, or teams, standing across from each other on the playing field. Each person on a team is assigned a number. Ideally there are even teams, with the same numbers on both sides. In the space between where the two teams are standing is the "bacon" (usually a flag or bandana). The adult with the group calls the numbers. It can be one number at a time or several numbers. If a player's number is called, he or she must run to the center of the field, pick up the bacon, and try to run it back to his/her line of teammates before being tagged by the person from the opposing team who has also run out to the center of the field because he or she has the same number. If the player makes it back to his or her team without getting tagged, then that team gets a point. If the player with the bacon gets tagged, no points are awarded. Usually play continues until a predetermined number of points is reached, or until most players are tired and thirsty. Then the winning team has first choice of beverages after playing.

Worm Tag

This activity can also be called "Octopus Tag," but, regardless of the name, the principles are still the same. One person is chosen as "it" (once again using the ratio of 15 players to 1 "it," though this may result in there being more than one "it" at a time). Boundaries are very important in this game, and those must be determined by the adult supervisor before the game begins. Whenever a player is tagged by the "it," the two people either link arms or hold hands. (Linking arms is preferred because holding hands can end up being sweaty and disgusting.) Once the two players are connected, they must work together to tag someone else, who then links arms with one of them. Once three or more players are linked, only the two people on the ends can tag people, while whoever is in the middle continues to run and remain connected with them. Play continues until everyone in the game is part of a worm.

Party Games

These types of games were long the province of children's birthday parties "back in the day." While some might think these activities would be of interest only to children because tweens would be far too "worldly" to want to play them, it instead seems that tweens embrace them and have a great time playing such games.

Hot Potato

This game can be played with or without music, but music is best. The idea is that everyone must sit in a circle and then pass the "potato" (some small object) around until the music stops. Whoever has the "potato" is now out. Usually the adult with the group is controlling the music, but that person must have his or her back turned so as not to bias when the music is stopped. Play continues until only one person is left. That person is the winner.

Murder

While the name of this game may be concerning to some adults, it is not violent at all. Everyone playing gets a card. Most of the cards are blank, but one has a D for "detective" and the other has M for "murderer." Once the players look at their cards, only the detective announces who he or she is. Then the detective leaves the room. Cards are collected and the lights are turned off. Everyone is supposed to mingle and talk to each other like they are at a party. The murderer, at any time, can tap his/her "victim" on the shoulder. Once the victim has been tapped, he or she should "die" as dramatically and loudly as possible. Once this happens everyone must freeze where they are, and the lights are turned on. The detective gets three guesses to figure out who the murderer is. There is no winning or losing—only dramatic deaths and stealthy murderers.

Musical Chairs

This is the classic party game in which chairs are set up in a circle for each participant minus one. Everyone walks around the chairs while the music plays. When the music stops, everyone must get a seat. The person left without a seat is now out. Play then continues with one chair removed. Each time the music stops, someone is out and another chair is removed. This goes on until only person is left and declared the winner.

Old School

There are some activities that do not have a specific category aside from being games that children and tweens happily played many years ago, and ones that current tweens do not seem to know much, if anything, about. The following games are definitely worth mentioning.

Seven Up

While this activity tends to be the province of classroom games, it bears mention for librarians. When doing school visits, there may be time to play a game, and this one is definitely a classic and still well loved. It is best to play with at least 20 people. Seven people are chosen to be "it." The next instructions are "heads down, thumbs up." Everyone puts their heads down on their desks or a table, and they make a fist with their thumb pointed up. Once everyone's eyes are covered, each "it" pushes down the thumb of one person. Once all the "its" have returned to their starting place at the front of the room, the adult calls, "Heads up. Seven up." Then the people whose thumbs have been pushed down stand up and take turns guessing who tagged them. If they guess correctly, they become "it" for the next game, and their tagger must sit down. Play continues indefinitely, or until it's time for another activity.

Jousting/Sword Fighting

There are many activities that 3-foot lengths of foam pipe insulation can be used for. Such instruments have served as swords for jousting when the summer reading theme was medieval, as well as lightsabers for *Star Wars* programming. The idea is that the tweens "do battle" with the foam pipe insulation but do not make physical contact with whoever they are fighting. When playing this game, two lines of tweens face each other. The instructions are to battle only the person directly across from them.

Outdoor Chalk Drawing

Having a large expanse of parking lot or sidewalk at the library can be a gift. For the price of a mega-box or two of sidewalk chalk, any size group of tweens can decorate whatever space is available. Typically there are tweens who say, "I don't know what to draw," and others who get started right away. Suggestions include drawing smiley faces and writing names in fancy script with lots of colors. There are always pairs of tweens who fill the space with tic-tac-toe boards. There will be a few tweens who decide to do chalk body outlines, as well as those who write "Johnny loves Suzy" messages. Do lay out whatever ground rules seem necessary for this activity, but, aside from that, just let them be creative. However, do not plan on saving much chalk from event to event. Usually the remaining chalk will be in small pieces or broken beyond use after a lengthy session of chalk art.

Pillow Fights

This was one tween advisory board's dearest desire for a while, although it took a bit of time to decide on a way to do this that would not result in injury but would still be fun. This activity is often proposed as part of larger programs like lock-ins. However, because of the cost involved in buying both pillowcases (which can be reused infinite times) latex balloons (which will have to be replaced for each event), it is not as inexpensive as many other "old-school" activities. Letting the tweens blow up two latex balloons per pillowcase (or, even better, having the balloons already blown up by staff or volunteers ahead of time, since most tweens do not know how to tie off a balloon) is the best method. It is safer not to let tweens bring their own pillows mostly because of varying pillow firmness. After all preparation are complete, arrange the tweens in two lines facing each other and let them beat the person across from them with their "balloon pillow"—this activity gets rave reviews each time it is done.

Water Balloons

There still seems to be magic in throwing water balloons at someone else. Whether it is a planned attack against an enemy (like the simulated wall of a simulated castle) or a free-for-all throwing event, tweens still love it. The challenge is that there are never enough pre-filled water balloons, no matter how many are prepared ahead of time. Sometimes tweens can fill the balloons themselves, but adults (or at least slightly older people) should be available to tie the knots in the balloons.

The Takeaway

While it may seem odd to offer some of these activities as part of library programs, it is in keeping with library's position as the preserver of cultural knowledge. Libraries hold all sorts of knowledge, but who teaches tweens how to play these games? There does not seem to be a clear-cut answer to this question anymore. Sometimes the answer is the library along with other places like home, school, and Scouting. It is also sometimes good for the library to provide tweens with some unstructured, creative time. Given the many activities modern tweens have going on, if even a short period of unstructured time can be offered for tweens to just be kids and run around and laugh, it is appreciated.

There really is no limit to what you can do with tweens because sometimes things that seem simple and old-fashioned are super popular and fun. There is nothing wrong with investigating different types of games and activities to play. Not everything has to cost a lot of money. Sometimes simple and low key is fun.

Here are some retro activities to remember for future programs:

- Chess
- Infection
- Sardines
- Go Fish
- Seven up
- Pillow Fight
- Musical Chairs
- Hot Potato

SECTION VIII

The Final Pieces for Successful Tween Services

This section covers all the information that does not fit anywhere else in this book, although much of it has been discussed indirectly throughout the preceding chapters. Specifically, this section formally covers marketing and outreach.

In the chapter about tween advisory boards, we describe the many things a tween advisory board can do to augment or make a tween librarian's job easier. In addition, this chapter will recap many of the suggestions that have made throughout this book regarding tween advisory boards. It cannot be said enough how significant they are, but such boards can be a challenge to create and maintain.

The marketing chapter will discuss different ways to market the library and its programs to tweens and their parents. Remember, there is no "one size fits all" rule when it comes to tweens; some of these strategies may work, and others may not. As always, any marketing campaign will need to be geared to the specific community in order to succeed.

The outreach chapter will cover different places that one can go to meet tweens outside of the library. However, committing oneself to be out in the community is a decision that must be made at the library. Is it a priority to reach tweens in the community, or is it better to concentrate almost solely on the tweens who come into the building? Do you even know what you want or what your library administration wants? These are important questions to answer before you look outside your library building.

In a way, these chapters tie everything else in this book together. All the different elements of tween services should be shared with the community in whatever ways seem best suited to reach them.

21

Your Tween Advisory Group

Maintaining a tween advisory group is a tricky task. Generally, it is not something that can be created by just putting an advertisement in the library newsletter and having it work perfectly after the first meeting. However, that does not mean that it cannot be done. It is something that needs to be approached deliberately and carefully.

Our first experience with tween advisory boards was back in 2010, when we started with six handpicked very young tweens. At this time, we are also offering an advisory group for children ages 4 to 8. Both groups were written about in an article about young advisory groups for IFLA: "Library Advisory Groups—Not Just for Adults and Teenagers Anymore!" (see http://www.ifla.org/files/assets/libraries-for-children-and-ya/newsletters/december-2010.pdf for the full article). Several other people have likewise written about tween advisory groups within the past few years, with a variety of suggestions for how to proceed.

Regardless of which pattern one chooses to follow, an advisory group is all about listening to kids. To truly know what is happening with the community's tweens, one must be willing to listen to them. Moreover, the tweens have to know that there is a willingness to listen without passing judgment. Tweens can tell when adults are judging them, and this instantaneously loses points with them. Tweens also expect that, if asked for their opinions, something will result from their answers. Asking for suggestions but not acting on them is practically a breach of trust. It is imperative to follow their suggestions, or at least have a good reason why doing so was not possible.

There is very little guidance that can be done with a tween advisory group. However, the whole meeting need not be a chaotic situation. Having an advisory group is about listening to the flow of ideas, watching how projects are completed, and absorbing the seemingly unrelated conversations that center on school or friends or community activities. Much can be learned from simple observation and listening.

Teen advisory groups have been going on for years, but having such a group specifically for tweens is a newer idea, but, then again, so is having specific services for tweens. Our tween advisory meetings are usually a half hour long, maybe forty-five minutes. Using a large whiteboard to write all the ideas, thoughts, and plans down in a mind map is a visual cue to the tweens that no idea is a bad idea. At the conclusion of the meeting, a picture is usually taken of the whiteboard so that everyone can remember all the different things that were suggested. Most of the participants are long-time library patrons whose parents know each other from bringing their children to the library for years. The parents sit and chat while the tweens work on whatever project is happening at the time. The fact that the parents make time for their tweens to participate says a lot about the relationship that has been created with both the tweens and their parents. As far as the tweens are concerned, they have certain expectations about what they will be doing. Whatever the task, they will be making a meaningful contribution to the library. It could be vetting new ideas for programs or materials that the librarians are considering, or it could be giving the librarians ideas. They expect to be asked questions until the librarians understand what they want, and they expect to have their questions answered by the librarians. There is trust between both groups, and it is built on mutual respect for each other and devotion to the library.

Many things can be done with tween advisory groups. Sometimes, in finding meaningful activities for them, one must think outside the box. One way to consider potential activities is to say to yourself, "What would I ask an adult patron help or advice about, or what might I ask another tween librarian about?" Usually this can help to find a way to scale these activities to the tween level. Some suggestions may be ridiculous, but if several ludicrous ideas all still seem to follow the same theme, then it may be necessary to find a way to incorporate these ideas into something that happens at the library.

Obviously some of the suggestions listed below will not work in your library, perhaps due to community size, staff size, unionization, or general divisions of labor within the library, but consider what you can do and just try things. We will move from the more traditional advisory activities to some more uncommon possibilities.

Program Planning

This category can include ideas for programs during the year or purely summer activities. Each library does programming its own way. Letting the tweens just throw out ideas of "cool things to do" can be a great way to get some suggestions. Not everything will be feasible in the library, but be open to their ideas. Also, ask them how they envision their program suggestion working in the library. It is like a reference interview: often what was perceived or extrapolated from the suggestion by the librarian is not anywhere close to what the tweens were actually talking about. In this book some of the previously discussed programs were different ideas that came from a tween advisory group, like the LEGO Club, live Pac-Man, pie fights, and pillow fights.

Summer Reading

In assisting with summer reading, the advisory group could help plan activities or choose prizes for the reading program. Learning what worthwhile incentives are for tweens can be invaluable. It can be as simple as finding local businesses that the tweens would like to get gift certificates or coupons from. Or, if everyone currently needs a cinch sak for school, one that just happens to have the library's logo on it could work out great as a summer prize.

No matter how seemingly silly the tweens' suggestions might be, write them down. Try to use them somehow. One year our tweens decided, in looking through the catalogs of inexpensive prizes that are available from different vendors, that plastic dog poop was something that many people would like to choose as a summer reading prize. While not the favorite choice of the parents, it was one of the first prizes to run out. Frequently the tweens provide all the seeds of ideas for programs during the summer to match with that year's summer reading theme. They like getting to write their ideas on the whiteboard, and they do seem to appreciate that we work hard to integrate as many of their ideas as possible into the final slate of programs.

Materials Selection

For us, the tween advisory group arose from materials selection. One very vocal early elementary school student thought we needed game guides for the Pokémon games he was playing on his Nintendo DS. His mother let him sit down with a librarian and look through the different books available from their book vendor to discuss what he was looking for and what he thought would be best for the library. Of course, this became a regular thing, and over the next year or two, every few months, when something new came out for Pokémon, then he would come to make sure the library had it on order. Of course, he told his friends, and eventually there were several children asking about Pokémon, *Star Wars*, and other media tie-in products.

Materials selection can take many different forms. In the context of an entire advisory group, getting advice on library materials can mean asking for ideas of favorite books and trying to make sure there are plenty of the actual titles (or similar titles) on the shelves. Our tween advisory group was the force behind the library getting Nintendo DS games to circulate. Some were advocating for this acquisition before there was even a formal group. Eventually, after finally convincing two different library staff members of the number of tweens they thought would borrow the games as well as a list of twenty-five titles to start out with, the library purchased its initial Nintendo DS collection.

Meeting with Book Vendors

This special activity only works with book vendors who are willing to accommodate the chaos that will inevitably ensue. Different salespeople handle things differently, but if any of the salespeople with whom the library works actually bring the books with them, having them meet with the tweens can be quite helpful. Tweens can reveal what kinds of topics are of interest to them as well as how they make their reading selections. We worked with a vendor for a while who brought books and had the tweens meet with him a few times. Each tween was given a pile of colored papers (one color per tween). If a tween found a book that he or she thought should go in the collection, then a colored paper was placed inside that book. The more papers were in a book, the more popular the tweens thought it would be, and the librarian was more likely to order it. Some tweens liked everything, but others put a lot of thought into their selections. Overall, this was a very quick process for the tweens. They made snap judgments based on the cover art or perhaps the information on the back cover. Some tweens chose items they were interested in personally, and others chose books that they knew their friends would like. For the vendor, it was a real experience because the tweens often chose books that he had not anticipated. He did not get to do much "selling" because the tweens were not interested—they knew what they wanted and what they did not.

Testing

Our tween advisory board frequently got the opportunity to test new equipment, program possibilities, or craft projects to see if they were something the librarians wanted to use again. Sometimes they had the opportunity to check out new items before they were put out for the rest of the library population. The tweens were excited to be the first to use the video game systems when we got them for the library. They played *Mario Kart* and, more important, generated a list of games the library needed to have people play. There was a lot of discussion about potential programs. The tweens were always brutally honest about what they thought.

Deaccession

Sometimes deaccession is fairly similar to weeding, but some libraries have a "last-chance" collection, which could include books that the librarian is about ready to weed from the collection but wants to give one last chance. The tween advisory board could provide the final vote on whether to remove those materials from the building. Asking for tween assistance in this area will give the staff valuable information on how the tweens evaluate materials, and listening to their rationales can be interesting. We have gone through this process several times with books meant for younger children. The books the tweens had to choose from were slated to be removed from the collection due to age and condition, or simply lack of circulation. The tweens went through the books and decided what should be kept, if anything. What was fascinating was that the reason for keeping something was frequently "someone might use it, but I don't like it." They were quite brutal with the books. There was none of the nostalgia over books that many adults can have. The tweens evaluated things as they saw them. They were also very clear about what they thought of books with dirty covers, yellowed pages, and otherwise "well-loved" books.

"Tidying Up"

Even seemingly mundane jobs can be interesting to the tweens if they feel it is an important part of caring for their library. This category can include straightening shelves, putting items back in alphabetical order, and other tasks of this nature. When a tween advisory board really gels, it tends to take a tremendous amount of personal pride and ownership in the tween section of the library. Having the tween board members help keep things tidy is a great way to continue to get buy-in for the tween section. We often had our tweens move sections of books from one shelving area to another. One staff member loaded the book cart, several tweens pushed it to the new location, and another staff member unloaded the books on their new shelves. The tweens loved pushing the carts—the heavier, the better. It was also extremely helpful for the librarians.

Website Design

The tweens at one point got the opportunity to do a video chat with the person redesigning the library website. Many of their ideas turned out to be about 6 or 7 years ahead of their time. Unfortunately, the labor cost to design their portion of the website was prohibitively expensive, and it was a good lesson for the tweens to discover how much things cost and how to make economical decisions. However, the most interesting thing about that experience was that what the tweens recommended a number of years ago is quite common in big commercial websites for tweens today. These tweens knew what they wanted. The other lesson gleaned from letting tweens participate in much larger library projects is that it can teach them about having to balance many different (and often conflicting) needs when making a decision.

Videography

Tweens love taking videos. Allowing them to use library equipment to make short movies promoting something about the library also fulfills tweens' need to be useful and make contributions. Tweens look for any reason they can think of to use our small, handheld video cameras. These flip cam–like devices have been used for a number of years. One project that the youths we work with are most proud of happened back in 2011, when the library was preparing for a levy campaign. The tweens went up to people in the library and asked them, "What do you like about your public library?" These clips were later edited together to make several short promotional videos for the library that were eventually used for the levy, as well as other times the library wanted to get its message out. The tweens interviewed their parents, their friends, people in the library that day, and even the staff. They received many different answers, and hardly anyone said no to being interviewed by a cute tween.

The Takeaway

Tweens want to be treated as adults, and they want to make significant contributions. Tween advisory groups give them the opportunity to make a positive impact on their library. They can also provide a wealth of knowledge; in essence, like a focus group, the advisory group can be used to obtain insider data on all things tween. However, that can only happen if the library staff with whom the tweens work view their ideas and contributions as significant. Tween advisory groups are about building on mutual respect of the participants and a shared love of the library.

22

Marketing to Tweens

Tweens are a constant marketing target. As discussed earlier, marketers are the groups who have studied tweens the most, seeking to learn how best to sell products to tweens. However, when marketing to tweens, it is also important to market to tweens' parents. Parents are still trying to have some influence over their tweens, and they need to be convinced that whatever is being advertised is a good idea. However, marketing the library in general and tween services in particular is something that must be done consciously and constantly.

Some of the most powerful marketing you can do with tweens and even their parents is not overt, like hanging a sign or passing out fliers. Anytime people working with tweens leave the library building, they should be branded (i.e., carrying something that clearly has the library's logo on it). This is different from just wearing a nametag, though wearing a nametag to put a name to a face is important in conjunction with branded clothing. Keeping the library's logo and name visible as often as possible is important when it comes to introducing tweens and other adults to the tween services librarians as well as the library in general. This means wearing a library polo shirt when shopping at the grocery store or even going to Wal-Mart to pick up supplies for a program. We have had wonderful interactions with many of the cashiers at our local Super Wal-Mart, which often ended up promoting the library. While this could seem counterintuitive, since Wal-Mart is big chain, the employees are local. They are part of the community, and they are frequently interested in what is happening at the library and why particular items are being purchased and whatever odd combinations of items are needed for an upcoming program.

Sometimes your duties as a tween librarian will include marketing yourself and, by extension, the library. Taking the opportunity to attend community events while wearing library-branded clothing is important. Helping at school functions to get yourself seen outside of the library is key, since you are reminding tweens and their parents that the library is an essential part of the community. You may have the opportunity to judge a local art contest, or you may choose to attend a performance of the middle school musical, thus showing that you care about all of the community's tweens, not just those you see in your library.

The other aspect of marketing as the tween librarian in the community is realizing that staff members are always ambassadors for the library, regardless of whether they are officially "on the clock." This is not to say that staff can never run to a home improvement store while wearing paint-covered clothes or they can never stop at the grocery store in sweatpants on the way home from the gym. This is more a question of how to conduct yourself overall, both in social media and in public, whether individually or as part of a group. Needless to say, the time for getting silly drunk at a local bar is done. No one wants a tween's parent to see you acting like that. And even if it is on your personal social media page and the post has nothing to do with work, do not post a hate-filled invective about a local or national political candidate; it does not paint you in the best light. You want tweens and their parents to feel comfortable being with you and know that you will behave responsibly and are open to all parts of the community.

Remember that your personal brand is forever. Unless you physically change the community in which you work, you will always be your library's tween librarian. You may get promoted to a branch manager or department head, but in the eyes of the tweens whom you worked with, you are still "their" librarian. Do not forget this. Your tweens may be out of college or bringing their own children to baby storytime, but you will always be the person they saw at the library. This is an awesome responsibility and common to any librarians who work with youths. However, it is important to mention here because the tween years are filled with such volatility that being a calm, encouraging, nonjudgmental presence in a tween's life will create a forever memory with them that you will need to honor forever.

When the opportunity arises to interact with tweens, do not talk down to them. Talking at and not to tweens is one of the fastest ways to lose credibility with this group. When marketing directly to them, they need to know that their intelligence and interests are appreciated and respected. Programs have to be described in an interesting, enticing way without ever pandering to tweens. If the program does not sound fun, no one is going to come. Book talks need to be honest and enthusiastic. The tween librarian also needs to stress that there are so many different books available that coming into the library is the best way to find something if none of the book talk subjects appeal to a particular tween. Do not tell a group that they will love everything that you have brought; they will not. Always be sincere and honest.

Personal selling is what you will do most often with tweens. It is often a mixture of being a carnival barker and the emcee of a sporting event. The goal is to get the tweens to buy into the library programs or services by the end of the presentation. When engaging the tweens, talk with them. If there are two people making the presentation, there should be give and take and some level of comedic repartee and respect between the presenters. The idea is to encourage the audience to engage with the presentation by cheering, clapping, and generally being enthusiastic about what is happening. If they are excited, they might remember the program and decide it is something that they absolutely have to do. This is buying the product.

Creating displays and more low-tech ways of marketing have their place even in the world of technology-absorbed tweens. A display about the library at a school function of some sort still has an impact. It is even better if, next to the display of tween-appropriate library activities, the tween librarian is standing there to answer questions and to greet the tweens. Another "old-fashioned" marketing technique is making fliers. Do not discount the usefulness of a sign on the library door or something on the inside of a bathroom stall. You always want people to know what is going on at their library for tweens. While handing out fliers in general, to tweens or parents, is probably not the most effective way to advertise, sometimes it is still worth doing. Unfortunately, the problem with fliers is that they get lost, and then the information on them is lost. In a similar vein, print newspapers are often only helpful for reaching grandparents in many communities; even online newspapers are not the first place many tweens or their parents turn to for information about what is happening in the community. Also, do not forget your library's volunteers, Friends groups, foundations, or governing bodies. These people need to be aware of what is going on and can be powerful supporters and sharers of information, as they will get asked vastly more often than you do about what programs are available in the library.

Social media in and of itself is an interesting challenge. The virtual locations where people gather change so fast that the information written in these sites will probably be inaccurate immediately after it is read. The other challenge with tweens is that some use certain social media because it's allowed by the sites; some use social media even when it's not officially allowed, and others do not use social media at all. You want to encourage tweens to connect with the library on social media, but it can be a delicate situation. Using Facebook, Twitter, Instagram, or whatever else is popular with local tweens is what you need to do. Keep an eye on what kids are talking about (and what their parents talk about). Also, if the tweens want a special place within a particular social media site for just their information, provide that. Listen to what they want. In addition, if the library has a specific page for tweens, make sure that the tweens' parents know and can use the page as well.

Encourage kids to share photos and videos of the library's activities on different social media platforms even if they do not acknowledge that they are at the library. Ask them to share awesome things they have done or been part of at your library. In many cases after lock-ins at our library, tweens started sharing videos that they took long before we even knew about it. We have also had some great success in the past with tweens as embedded videographers. Often tweens are handed an inexpensive digital video camera during a program with the aim of letting them record what they see. These videos, shot by tweens in the moment, can be the best marketing tools because they often have a viral element to them, and the tween videographers are eager to share their work (and other tweens are interested in seeing what they have done).

Letting tweens have some control over the marketing of "their area" is important. Many of them take a lot of pride in the videos they make, and they want their work to be available for everyone to see. The role of the library staff in these situations is editing—that is, making as much of the video useable and viewable as possible. The primary thing to consider with this task is, of course, privacy. Make sure that if you are allowing tweens to take videos or photographs, and certainly if you or another member of the library staff is doing it, whatever permissions the library requires for releasing photos and videos are taken care of. If you do have tweens who cannot have photos or videos taken of them, they may be great candidates to be your videographers.

Among other things, reach out to "alpha tweens and alpha tween parents." These people will talk tween services up to their friends and hopefully gain the library more support in the community. These are important people to know, and you want them to know that you appreciate what they have done to help you. These individuals may or may not be in your library Friends group or part of some other group directly tied to the library. You want these people supporting your activities and sharing them with their personal social networks. Getting their endorsement can bring a lot of support and attention to what you are doing for tweens in the library.

There are other ways of getting information out to people. Slider scripts on library webpages as well as on social media can be used to show image advertisements for program and services. Also, if the library collaborates with other groups in the community to provide programming or services of some kind, encourage them to talk about their partnership with the library on their own social media and other marketing outlets. The library will reach a whole lot more people that way. Nor should you discount local newsletters and calendars that cover multiple groups' activities. Using a mixture of online and "old-school" marketing will create the greatest impact.

Summer reading is a huge part of youth services librarianship, and you always want to have as many participants as possible for this annual event. Marketing summer reading to tweens can be a bit different from marketing to other kids. Sometimes it is all about the prizes. While it would be better to encourage reading for the love of reading, depending on the community it may be better to emphasize "awesome prizes." Donated prizes are great, but if it is necessary to buy them, investing in and buying things from places where tweens like to shop is going to give you an extra edge and attraction. These can be places that are typically associated with malls, like Hot Topic or Claire's, as well as specialty stores like Build-A-Bear or GameStop. Items or gift cards from these stores are always good prizes to work toward or use as raffle prizes. However, with this said, shop locally whenever possible. You are going to meet important people who might be able to help publicize your programs to potential attendees if you talk to the salespeople while you are getting what you need. You never know whom you might meet or who may be able to help you.

Amid all of the suggestions offered in this chapter, do not forget to try any new ideas you think of on your own. There may be new, different, and successful ways to market and reach out to tweens in your community. These are our ideas. They are not the only ways. Be adventurous and try things.

Much of this chapter is devoted to marketing to patrons outside the library, but we would be remiss if we did not also focus on patrons who are already in the library. It is often assumed that the patrons who frequent the library are already knowledgeable and have a full understanding of what is going on and what they can be a part of. Often this is where libraries fail when trying to reach patrons. Never assume a regular patron knows everything that is available at the library. For example, making small talk with tweens and their parents while looking for materials is an excellent way to promote upcoming programs. Having fliers available in various locations that can be handed to patrons as a reminder can be extremely useful. A great use of in-building technology is to use the library computer screensavers to show image advertisements for programs and services.

Additionally, do not forget to market tween programs to the other library staff members. In many cases the circulation staff will see more parents and tweens than the rest of the professional staff. Often these staff members know a great deal about the patrons they see on a regular basis and may know who has a tween in their lives who might want to attend a program or use a service. Getting circulation and other library staff members knowledgeable and excited about tween programing and services can be an excellent marketing tool.

The Takeaway

Marketing is important. It is not something to just hope will happen on its own. It takes effort, regardless of whether you have someone in your library who is specifically there to do marketing.

Some things to remember:

- You are a representative of the library everywhere you go. You *are* tween services, so you should behave as such.
- Old-school "personal touch" marketing can be very successful, and you must be willing to do it anytime.
- Use the social media tools that your tweens and their parents most talk about. Meet them where they are virtually.
- Encourage tweens and their parents to market the library themselves to their own groups of friends.
- Do not forget to market to the patrons within your building. Do not assume they know what services and programs are available.
- Do not forget to keep other staff, especially circulation staff, current with library programs and services. They may be one of the best ways to market tween programs and services.

23

Outreach

You have researched, investigated, and planned the perfect tween programs, collection, and services for your community. If you build it, they will come, correct? Unfortunately, that is seldom the case. You must go out into the community to find the tweens, rather than waiting for them to come to you. However, enticing tweens to come to the library is not the only purpose for outreach in the community. Since tweens are frequently completely dependent on adults in their lives for transportation, they may want to come to the library but cannot. It is primarily for these tweens that you do outreach. Outreach tweens deserve to have a library experience even if they cannot actually come to the library.

Outreach and marketing have plenty of overlaps when it comes to being outside the library and representing the library. It should be understood that while outreach has a specific goal and purpose, whenever staff are outside the library they are always ambassadors for the library and tween services. Thus, marketing is an integral part of outreach, and while not every patron can be persuaded to come to the library, an effort should always be respectfully made.

If possible, two people should be part of any outreach effort. Sometimes this can be perceived as overkill or squandering staff time when the outreach event is not physically demanding. However, there is safety in numbers. This is not meant to imply that leaving the library building is itself unsafe, but it does mean that having multiple "faces of the library" available to see tweens in particular, as well as any other community group, is better in the long run. You want multiple people who are known presences to represent the library because someday one of them will have a conflict with another activity or be unable to go due to illness. It is best to have a diverse stable of people who can be out in the community talking to tweens and their parents about how amazing the library's tween services are. Referring to the many tween archetypes mentioned earlier in this book, different staff people will be able to appeal to and communicate with the different archetypes. Having multiple staff members at an outreach location also takes the pressure off and allows multiple people to handle parts of the outreach event as well as answer questions, prepare materials, and meet and greet with tweens and their adults.

Additionally, making outreach trips often requires the movement of equipment and resources like book talk materials and marketing materials. Having extra hands to share the load not only is sensible but also will save on the wear and tear of the above resources as well as the outreach staff.

Outreach to the Schools

There are many ways you can increase visibility for your tween programs in schools. There are the more traditional ways of being in the schools, like holding book talks or doing summer reading promotion in the form of skits or presentations of some kind. Tweens have been seeing both of these activities since they were very young. As children become tweens, their book talks should become more serious. It is about the content of the book, not just the glitz and showmanship of selling the product. To promote summer reading to elementary school students, skits and presentations are frequently campy or over the top, but for tweens the sell is more straightforward. While the goal is to have the tweens be excited, it is best to be more honest about the fact that we are trying to persuade them to participate in the program. Remember to talk *to* the tweens and not *at* them, even in large groups and assemblies; even if the only thing that tweens remember is that you come to the school every year to talk about summer reading, you will have made an impact. Also, remember that there are other ways to reach the schools—for example, find out whether your programs can be included as part of the school announcements each day. If the announcements are televised, can you be interviewed as part of the program? Is it possible to do a short monthly book talk as part of the announcements? Can you post fliers in the students' common areas or have fliers sent home? Can the library get access to the school's SIS (student information system) and post messages and fliers for the parents there? Can you have a book discussion group meet during lunch or study hall?

Beyond the very blatant marketing techniques mentioned above, there are more subtle ways to market the library by reaching out to the schools. One of our favorite approaches is finding school-based groups or programs that need adult volunteers. This goes beyond the typical reading assistance program and is more like parent-teacher groups, sports groups, drama club, or any number of other entities. You could even chaperone a dance or a field trip. This is the time to find out who on your library staff is connected with the schools and get them to introduce you to people who can get you in the schools. Meet with the principals and teachers. Bring brownies to an all-building staff meeting. (Baked goods—preferably homemade, not store-bought—are almost always welcome for school staff.) Offer to help at any of the school's evening events like open houses, meet-the-teacher events, literacy nights, or anything that would allow you to meet more people. Sometimes you will have the option of being at one of these events with fliers and information about the library, but most of the time you will be there in your library polo shirt schlepping stuff or doing whatever needs to be done.

Section VIII. The Final Pieces for Successful Tween Services

We will mention a couple of our favorite programs in our community, and hopefully that will spark your thought processes for things that might be similar where you are. The middle school in our community participates in Junior Achievement. At least two library staff members (preferably more) participate in the "Blitz Days," when for several hours members of the community come into the school to talk about financial literacy. We have been doing this for a number of years, and many tweens in the community will say, "I remember you from Junior Achievement." That is awesome, and the other nice thing is that Junior Achievement does not seem especially library-like to these tweens. It gives the library staff an opportunity to interact with the tweens and get to know them in a different context.

A few years back it seemed like one of the schools we wanted to visit was not inviting us in as readily as we would like. After talking with some of the tweens' parents whom we know quite well, we were invited by them to come to the school to help with various PTA activities. The PTA always needed assistance with different things like book fairs, Santa's Workshop, or ice cream socials. While we did not really talk about the library at any of these events, we were there in our polo shirts (usually serving food) to the groups of tweens, children, and parents who attended. We cannot tell whether our relationship with this school changed because the officers of the PTA invited us in or whether things changed with the passage of time. However, we were introduced by more tweens to their parents when we were helping the PTA than at practically any other community event.

When you go to the school to do the typical hard sell, you have to determine what groups you will see and speak to. Sometimes you are selling the children on your programs; other times you are selling the parents. For example, when you go to an after-hours program at one of the schools, you are typically selling to the parents, and, if possible, you are selling them on both tween and adult programs. We often show up with a tri-fold display with full-sheet ads for our programs and services available for whatever ranges of people we think we might see. We usually bring our own tablecloth with the library logo on it and send at least two staff members, so that if one staff member is engaging a parent, the other is ready to help or greet another tween. Always remember that you and the people who go out into the community with you are often community celebrities. Meeting and greeting is part of the marketing and outreach you need to do.

Other Community Venues

Tweens, like their younger siblings, may not be independently mobile. Depending on your community, you might have to do more convincing of the people in charge of transportation that it is important to come to the library. But when it comes to collections and services in the library, you probably need to reach the tweens themselves more. However, when this approach does not yield the successes you want, you need to decide how and where you are going to bring library services to the tweens.

In our case, we work quite a bit with two afterschool care facilities that also provide daylong care in the summer. These tweens have parents who work quite a bit, and often they cannot make it to the library. When we go to these facilities, we are the library for these tweens. They are so excited and appreciative of anything we do. We have worked with the summer programs at these facilities for almost ten years each. At first, the same programs offered at the library were transported and replicated at these facilities. For the last few years, however, we have done separate programs for them that better fit their facilities and the interests of the tweens who are there. In the last three years, we have gotten grant funding solely to invest in supplies for programs at these two facilities in the summer. These two groups have summer reading come to them. The tweens can borrow books and receive their summer reading prizes for reaching certain levels over a period of time. Borrowing books is the most important thing to these tweens. Many of them do not have library cards, and what we bring each week is all they know of the library. We have a boxmobile that allows us to offer circulation outside the building. (See our Public Libraries Online blog post at http://publiclibrariesonline.org/2015/11/boxmobile-the-bookmobile-alternative/ for more details.) We also use a limited-access card for the tweens during the summer so they can borrow some library materials, but the library assumes the financial burden if the materials are lost or damaged. Very few have been lost over the couple of years that we have been circulating materials. And the rewards in tweens' happiness and their joy at choosing and reading their own books more than make up for the time and effort it takes to haul the books and other necessary materials around.

Personal Introductions to New Groups

It cannot be said enough, whether in reference to the schools or other groups in the community: Make use of your library staff and have them bring you to the attention of people within groups in your community that you want to market to. They can do this by personally introducing you or using their social media outlets to spread the word about things you have going on. In a sense, social media can be like outreach, even though most people tend to think of it more in a marketing sense. Each of your colleagues has a different circle of friends, and if they are willing to share information on what you have available for tweens, you might reach any number of people. Also, make sure that the people who work at the circulation desk or the reference desk (whether these are multiple locations or the same place) have information on what is available in the library for tweens. These people can be some of your biggest cheerleaders and supporters; you just need to give them information. As we have stated before, this is where both marketing and outreach blend together.

The other thing to do is ask to go to outreach events that other colleagues in your building attend. Getting into different arenas to meet people is always a good idea. You never know who you will meet somewhere completely unrelated to tweens who will be able to help spread your message about the awesome things you are doing. Ask about attending chamber of commerce events, rotary meetings, band boosters, or local government meetings. There are many places where you could make a connection.

The Takeaway

There are many ways to reach out to tweens and other adults in the community. Outreach and marketing go together, so some techniques are the same. However, taking every opportunity to represent the library in the community, whether overtly talking about library services or quietly wearing the library's logo, is important.

Our favorite outreach ideas are:

- becoming an adult volunteer at the schools either through the PTA or through some other organization;
- being in the schools as often as you can to promote the library;
- finding other places in the community where you can meet tweens and perhaps be the library for them; and
- getting help from colleagues to meet people from other community groups with whom you might be able to share the message of available tween services.

Conclusion

What Have We Learned So Far? What Did We Wish We Could Do Differently?

You are never done with planning and tweaking your tween services model. Tween services are not as stationary as either children's services or those for young adults. The age range might need to change or the mix of books may not be right. There is always something that can be adjusted.

Being a tween librarian can be a lonely business. While there are two of us collaborating at our own library, that's not always the case for colleagues elsewhere who will be serving tweens along with some other age group. Sometimes even when there are two of us, it can still seem lonely because we feel separate from the other folks who offer programs for the library. We don't really belong in a particular area; for tween services, you borrow from the programming ideas of several different age groups. In some instances, the tween collection and service area may be physically located apart from the rest of the staff. Additionally, if the geographic area isn't ready to focus on tween services, you may not find as many other librarians in the vicinity who are equally passionate about this age group.

For us, what we wished we would have known is how much concentrated effort developing tween services takes. Each of us has many other responsibilities at the library because it is a small, standalone facility. If even one of us could have devoted our full attention to tween services, it might have been less scattered and haphazard, at least in the beginning.

Developing a good understanding of the community is imperative. We surveyed and analyzed as we were in the midst of building our program, and it really does need to happen first. Learn how the community views itself. If you analyze the community and come to certain conclusions that don't match how the community views itself, then tread lightly. Use the information thus gathered to inform your decisions, but don't discount people's beliefs about the community in which they live. Often historical perceptions do not match the current demographics but are firmly entrenched in patrons' minds, and this shapes their perceptions.

Also, getting buy-in from administration and coworkers is vital. We were quite lucky to have a number of staff members interested in different aspects of tween

Conclusion

library services, but making the case for why this group is central to the entire library and the library's continuum of service is critical for long-term success.

Finally, we would have reached out to other librarians outside our building sooner than we did. We didn't find many people who seemed interested in tween services at first, and we didn't try as hard as we should have to cultivate connections with other librarians. As we write this book about tween services, we have been lucky to have some of our colleagues provide suggestions and feedback about what we have written. We are so fortunate to have supportive library friends, and, unsurprisingly, some of these friends are young adult librarians and children's librarians, while others are in administrative or other roles.

To wrap up this book, we want to say thank you to all the northeast Ohio librarian colleagues who have helped us along the way in our careers, and thank you to some amazing tweens who inspired our interest in this age group. If we hadn't met these tweens, we might not have become so passionate about this subject.

Index